BE HAPPIER THAN THE DALAI LAMA

THE WISDOM OF THE GREAT MASTERS APPLIED TO THE MODERN WORLD

José Antonio Manchado

BE HAPPIER THAN THE DALAI LAMA

THE WISDOM OF THE GREAT MASTERS APPLIED TO THE MODERN WORLD

Be happier than the Dalai Lama.
The wisdom of the Great Masters applied to the modern world
José Antonio Manchado

Edited by:
PUNTO ROJO LIBROS, S.L.
Cuesta del Rosario, 8
Sevilla 41004
Spain
902.918.997
info@puntorojolibros.com

Printed in Spain * European Union
ISBN: 9788416439492

Layout and production: Punto Rojo Libros
Cover design: Vanesa Rodríguez
Translation: Alexia Weninger and Rubén Pérez

To Julia Rivas, for her help and support during the preparation of this book.

Contents

Introduction and acknowledgements

*Thousands of candles can be lighted from a single candle, and the life
of the candle will not be shortened. Happiness never decreases by being shared.*

Buddha

I dedicate a large part of my life to giving workshops and seminars on personal discovery, well-being, reconnecting with life and finding true happiness. In these activities I often use anecdotes and experiences I have had the blessing of having or witnessing, as a way to illustrate with real-life examples the various teachings I want to share, such as overcoming challenges, managing fears, discovering your true self and learning to live in peace and with full awareness.

Some time ago, patients, students and friends started suggesting that I write a book, to make all of these experiences accessible to more people. So one fine day I made the decision to gather some of them together and make them available to all beings without exception.

While all of the situations described in this book are real, and are the fruit of my own experiences, they do not appear in chronological order: I opted to focus instead on the teachings themselves, on the message that can be drawn from them, and on the exercises of peace and mental clarity, intuitively choosing as examples the experiences that seemed most illustrative. Most of the stories are accompanied by a reflection from the masters and some type of practice activity. In others readers are simply encouraged to quietly connect with how they feel after reading the text.

I would like to emphasize that, despite its title, this book is not purely Buddhist, nor is it about the Dalai Lama, although I certainly have great respect and admiration for him and his work in raising awareness and spreading the teachings of Dharma and peace all over the world.

This book, thanks to the wide variety of masters that have guided and inspired me, contains the essence of many philosophies and spiritual paths, so I invite you to open your heart and read it independently of any label or concept, with the understanding that all paths are rivers leading to the same ocean.

The intention behind the writing of this book is to build a bridge between ancestral tools and the modern world in which we live. Although the teachings explored here are based —at a profound level— on unity and therefore tend to use non-dualistic language, in this book you will find dual language, or language at different levels... Let me clarify: my priority is to make something easy and practical out of a topic that might at first seem complicated and suitable only for a few "fortunate ones". I wanted to write a book that could be understood by any reader, regardless of the previous knowledge he or she may have. I decided, therefore, that the reflections I offer should maintain the level of awareness I had when these situations occurred in my life, and to renounce form in favor of content, because I know in my heart that the true way to comprehend these teachings is through practice and direct experience.

What you will read and, if you wish, practice in this book will help you "deprogram" a mind that has been "programmed" in conflict, so that you can experience a state of genuine, unconditional and true peace.

To conclude this introduction, I would like to express my profound gratitude to all the beings who have inspired this book and have helped me learn to "deprogram" my mind (eliminating the limiting beliefs programmed into it) and thus be able to remember, reawaken and attain this state of joy and understanding in my life. Thank you to all my friends, students and the over one thousand patients I have treated and, particularly, to teachers such as Kalu T and Mr. Díaz, and countless other extraordinary persons who have enabled me to learn and remember the meaning of life. And, of course, a huge THANK YOU, in capital letters, goes to my family: my father and my mother, who are among my greatest teachers and whom I love unconditionally.

My deepest thanks to all of you!

May the teachings of this book benefit all beings without exception!

José Antonio Manchado

Chapter 0

"Expecting an intellectual understanding of Buddhist texts alone to solve our problems is like a sick person hoping to cure his or her illness through merely reading medical instructions without actually taking the medicine".

Geshe Kelsang Gyatso

In my early encounters with my teachers, when I saw and felt their smiles and eyes full of joy, I had the strange sensation (like many Westerners do) that for some reason they knew some "joke" that I could not quite perceive.

On one occasion, when I spoke to them of what I considered my problems, one of these teachers commented that life is one big, wonderful joke and the only challenge is to understand it so that you can laugh along with it.

I asked him to please share it with me. And he responded like this:

I will show you some practices aimed at revealing your true nature that will help you discover the illusory nature of what you call "problems". This true essence is like an immense shining sun and, to connect with it, all you need to do is sweep away the clouds of ignorance that are covering it.

Today, after experiencing what these wise people have shared with me, I smile with a feeling of true happiness, knowing that I am ONE with life. The tools are simple and I share them every day; many of them have been gathered together in this book.

Let us now begin the journey that will reunite us with our true happiness...but please remember:

"I have no absolute truths, nor definite answers. In fact, I know absolutely nothing.

All I have are the experiences I have gone through and felt. Don't believe anything you hear me say.

Just apply some of these tools that have worked for me and for others, and then share your experience with all other beings without exception".

José Antonio Manchado
The yoga of happiness workshop January 2012, Lanzarote.

Chapter 1: How it all started

"Goodbyes are only for those who love with their eyes.
Because for those who love with heart and soul, there is no such thing as separation".

Rumi

In 1995 something happened that would end up triggering a drastic change in my life. I was nineteen when my paternal grandfather, for whom I felt great affection and admiration, suddenly became ill. His health worsened by the day, and his suffering intensified to the point that his daily routine was a constant battle against pain. Soon he had to be admitted to the hospital.

I informed my family that I would not be going to visit him: I wanted to remember him as the strong, happy and serene man that he was. With the degree of consciousness I had at the time, I adamantly refused to let my mind's final image of my grandfather be that of an old man consumed by pain.

However, the twists and turns of life often do not take into account one's resistances, however firm they may be, and that day an unexpected complication arose: I needed the family car for something urgent, but my father had taken it to the hospital. To get the keys, I had no choice but to go up to that cold hospital room in which an old man writhing in pain, who physically had very little to do with the man my grandfather had once been, was screaming and raving, holding tight to the sheets of the hospital bed in which he would die shortly thereafter. That was, at that point in my life, a very disturbing image that stayed etched in my memory for many years.

Curiously enough, that same year the grandfather of a friend of mine also passed away. This elderly gentleman decided to gather all of his loved ones together on a Saturday afternoon. While comfortably reclining on his bed, he called the members of the family in one by one: he smiled affectionately at each of them, he gave them some words of advice and, after speaking with my friend's mother last of all, he said:

—Now I can go in peace.

He smiled and, as he exhaled his last breath, he allowed himself to die peacefully.

These two contrasting ways of saying goodbye to the world had such an impact on me that a question began to rise up inside me: how can it be that one person can die with so much resistance and pain, while another dies with such harmony, even happiness. I began to have the strange sensation that there was something I had not been told.

Thanks to these two events, I began a search and started down a path on which numerous encounters and experiences would help shed light and understanding on this whole matter.

Story:

—What is it that your master teaches? —asked a visitor—. Nothing —responded the disciple.

—Then why does he give talks?

—The only thing he does is point the way. He doesn't teach anything.

This seemed incomprehensible to the visitor so the disciple explained:

—If our teacher taught, we would transform his teachings into beliefs. But our teacher is not interested in what we believe, only in what we see.

Anthony de Mello

Chapter 2: The search

"Buddhism is more than a religion. It is a science of the mind".

Dalai Lama

"Without direct experience, the teachings become intellectual talk or a mere collection of new things to learn and will not make any real sense or effect any changes in our lives".

Tenzin Wangyal Rinpoche

After the experience I had during my grandfather's illness and death, a burning desire to learn the answers to the questions I felt growing inside me prompted me to attend a number of lectures, courses, workshops and talks about very diverse and different religions, philosophies, beliefs, spiritual tendencies... But none of them truly resonated for me.

For some reason, the unmoving, dogmatic, dualist and overly abstract concepts, the supposed laws and codes that people were asked to blindly obey, the rigidity of rules and rites, the constant search outside of oneself... all of this clashed with my simple and natural way of approaching life. I did not want to live burdened with fear and guilt, nor did I want to struggle to repress my feelings, and certainly not to deny primordial aspects of LIFE (with capital letters), in exchange for obtaining eternal salvation, or under the threat of burning in hell's flames for all eternity! Was somebody really going to reward me for leading a monotonous, taciturn, guilt-ridden life, after living through an old age of suffering, conflict and decrepitude? Had God really created fear, guilt and suffering?

In contrast, I also came across masters who simply said:

—Do nothing! You mustn't do anything at all, because this is all just a dream.

But they were forgetting that to reach that point experientially and not just conceptually, they themselves had had to spend many years meditating or practicing and so I felt, at least for a person in my situation, that some tools for beginners were needed, to help me first "deprogram" my mind so closely identified with what is false (the ego) that I was always looking for happiness outside, in the world around me. If this weren't the case, Buddha probably would not have "bothered" to transmit over eighty thousand teachings to help us discover our true nature.

Then I was blessed to come across on my path various Tibetan Buddhist monks and lamas, teachers of meditation and mental calm, wise people of different traditions, and sound therapists... All of these people offered me answers, adapting their language and practices to the level of consciousness I had at the time. They gave me an array of tools and pointed me towards a clear path that would help me gradually understand, "deprogram" and learn, little by little, to access my inner silence, past all thoughts, and connect with the universal wisdom that is beyond all concepts and limits. This path has led me to witness on some occasions, and to experience first hand on other occasions, different stories that have come to fill me with understanding, creating space and freedom inside me. These are the stories I now want to share with you, along with some practices and reflections from these great masters who have learned how to live in a state of unconditional happiness and well-being, connected with their true nature.

Each and every one of the people and experiences appearing in this book are real. However, for reasons of privacy and personal circumstances, some of them have asked me to change or omit their names, or their geographical location, because they want to remain peacefully anonymous.

Author's note:

The following chapters include practices and reflections considered by my teachers to be "pre-sadhanas" (prior to the awakening). Once we have become awakened to our true nature, all searching ends and we proceed to deepen our experience of Unity.

By observing how the masters respond to different situations and challenges, we can gain great insight towards a conscious attitude to life, making every experience an opportunity to reencounter truth, where your own "Inner Master" resides.

Story:

There is a story about a lama who always insisted on the importance of perceiving emptiness. He encouraged all the monks and Dharma practitioners to empty themselves of everything and perceive the empty substrate of all phenomena. He spent so much time emphasizing the need for emptiness that one day some monks went up to him and said:

—Venerable lama, we do not wish to question your teachings in any way but we would like to know why you place so much emphasis on the doctrine of emptiness. Can you please tell us?

The lama smiled and asked them to meet with him at sundown, instructing them each to bring a Tibetan bowl full of water. At nightfall, the monks went to the temple with their bowls with water, and the teacher said:

—Gently hit the bowl and make it sound. I want to hear the music of these singing bowls.

The monks did as they were asked, but the sound was dull and muffled. The lama then said:

—Now empty your bowls and make them sound again.

The monks obeyed. This time the sound was excellent, alive, enveloping and in expansion! The lama exclaimed:

—Do you see it now? A full bowl makes no sound! In emptiness you will find all the wisdom and truth of the Universe. All you have to do is empty yourselves like you did the bowls.

Chapter 3: Fear

"Overcome fear and behold in wonder how your world is transformed".

Aeschylus of Eleusis

"Love casts out fear and, conversely, fear casts out love.
And not only love. Fear also casts out intelligence, casts out goodness, casts out all
thought of beauty and truth, and all that remains is desperation. In the end, fear
casts out even a man's humanity".

Aldous Huxley

I have always loved being close to the sea, so it comes as no surprise that surfing is one of my great passions. For me it is a unique way to meditate in motion and feel that I am one with nature. When I was young I took any chance I had to get away from it all and surf in the waters of this marvelous island in the Atlantic, Lanzarote.

One day when I was 19, shortly after the death of my grandfather, I was surfing in La Santa, a beautiful spot on the western side of the island. It was a spectacular winter day, the waves were huge; so much so that only a few of us, the most adventurous, dared to get into the water. Even so, I was totally relaxed and alert: I knew where to go and I was able to comfortably slide over those incredible masses of water. I remember that about thirty people were watching us from the shore. Everything was wonderful until suddenly, something changed. I remember it as if it were a film flashing before my eyes in slow motion.

The first thing I noticed was the sun clouding over. Then I heard whistles and horns honking. I understood that something was happening: people were trying to warn us that some type of danger was imminent. Then I saw them. A series of waves, alarmingly large, was approaching us. My situation was especially tricky, because, if I didn't do something quickly, the first wave would break right above me, crashing over my body. I knew I had to stay calm and row quickly toward the wave, to either try to surf it or go under it in a duck dive.

I was just about to reach the wave when I saw another surfer coming out of it, speeding straight at me and completely out of control. I yelled at him with all my strength to try to avoid the blow of his surfboard on my head and, fortunately, I was able to swerve away. However, I ended up in an even worse situation: I was at the mercy of that monstrous wave and had no air in my lungs. An instant later I received the tremendous lashing of that wave, which crashed over me with the force of a speeding train and sent me straight to the bottom. The blow was so strong that I felt my shoulder dislocate and at the same time I realized that the tether to my surfboard was twisted around my neck.

All I could see was white foam: I didn't know where the surface was, which way was up or down, or where my arms and legs were. I only felt the pressure around my neck and the suffocating feeling of being unable to breathe.

In a situation like that, the smartest thing to do is to not struggle and to let yourself be dragged down by the sea, because any effort, even the slightest one, represents a loss of energy, of air and of time. I knew that a wave of that size would keep me under the water for at least one full minute and right then one minute was an eternity, especially knowing that that shout of warning to the other surfer had left me with no air whatsoever in my lungs.

I don't know how it happened. I only remember that I managed to free myself of the tether that was squeezing my neck, and thus release the pressure on my throat. I managed to reach the surface and get a little gulp of air, which helped me withstand the two raging blows that followed the first one. The worst was over. I climbed onto my board and, gripping it tightly, let myself drift towards the rocky shore. There several friends were waiting to help me.

I remember my entire body hurting, the marks on my neck, the bluish tone of my lips, face and hands. I felt my heart racing, as if it were going to explode inside my chest. I looked in panic at the sea, the same sea that I had loved so much since childhood. And I could not reconcile these two conflicting feelings.

When I arrived home I was determined to give up the sport that had always thrilled me, to never surf again. Just thinking about the sea brought a feeling of great pressure to my chest and made me breathless.

Around that time I met Ángel, an excellent martial arts instructor and a great meditator. When I told him my story, he said:

—Manchado, my friend, go surfing again. Choose a day when the sea is, at the very least, as rough as it was that fateful day.

I thought he was joking, that he hadn't listened to my story or that he had gone completely insane. The mere thought of returning made my entire body shake. I explained that I couldn't do that, that the mere thought of me surfing again made my heart stop. To this he responded:

—No, my dear friend. If you are unable to overcome that fear, then your heart has already stopped, because a fear you don't overcome turns into a prison and steals your life. The sea is a great passion of yours. Are you going to sacrifice that because of one unpleasant experience? It is sad to see how every day we decide to put an end to our dreams, our projects, our passions (in short, to everything that makes us feel good) because of a bad experience. You need to understand that there is such a thing as biological fear, a survival instinct that keeps you alive: it prevents you from driving the wrong way down a one-way street, from putting your fingers in an electrical socket or jumping off a cliff without a parachute. But there is also such a thing as psychological fear, or toxic fear, a fear that conditions you and makes your life become limited. What you are feeling towards the sea is a limiting and unnecessary fear. Before the accident, you surfed big waves. Waves even bigger than that one! Go back, Manchado, and take back what is rightfully yours.

It took me three weeks to digest all this. Then one day I heard that a big storm was heading toward the island and would bring enormous waves. When the time came, I went to the northeastern part of the island, where the sea around Lanzarote is the most violent when the weather gets rough. While I drove I noticed that I felt short of breath and my legs were trembling. When I reached my destination and saw the usual surf scene on the shore, my heart started racing. In the distance I saw great sets of waves of terrifying strength and size, which did not help me at all in my effort to stay calm! In fact, I couldn't remember having ever seen anything like it.

I parked a short distance away, so that I wouldn't be bothered by any of my surfer friends there that day, who would no doubt have come up to me to ask how I was doing. While I put on my wetsuit, I felt my heart way up in my temples, and it was beating faster and faster. I thought it was going to break through my chest! I felt like I might faint. However, I let myself have all these feelings, I got in the water and went towards the waves. I had to row with only my right arm because my left arm was completely paralyzed.

My first wave appeared before me, a monster at least three meters high. Instinctively, I went under it and, as I did so, the following thoughts came calmly and naturally into my head: "I am like a dolphin. I am part of the ocean. This is where I've spent some of the best times of my life. This is my home". I can't explain what happened there. It was as if that wave washed away all of my fears, as if it swept my body and mind clear of all traces of fear, as if the panic had never existed. My heartbeat returned to normal. My body returned to a state of calm. That afternoon I spent at least two hours surfing nonstop. My fear had disappeared entirely.

What do the masters say?

Fear, if such a thing exists, is nothing but a survival instinct the purpose of which is to protect us from or prepare us for some challenge or danger. The problem comes when we take it to the mental, psychological or imaginary level, where it turns into something toxic that conditions our life, shaping it with catastrophic or painful expectations that something bad will happen to us.

At a deeper level, these masters understand that fear is not real. It is the creation of a reactionary mind, which tends to always feel it is under attack or in conflict. In fact, the masters have an interesting suggestion for an experiment. They ask that you observe the physical and emotional symptoms you had in a situation of great danger, a moment in which you felt very afraid, and then compare these symptoms with the ones you felt when you were about to have your first kiss... You will find there is no difference between them, the only thing that varies is your expectation, your interpretation of the two events!

Fear means you are either in the past, remembering an experience deemed unpleasant or undesirable, or in the future, thinking that something bad or harmful is going to happen. But if we are in the present, living the here and now, there can be no fear.

Fear is an emotion that manifests when we enter areas of uncertainty: when, in some aspect of our life, our beliefs register something new, we react by feeling afraid.

Love is freedom; fear is the opposite.

Fear is a lack of confidence in life and in ourselves.

Fear is a distortion of reality, a projection of our reactionary mind living in the absence of love. And in such a state, we believe we are going to be attacked.

Fear is a great indicator that shows us how attached we are to a situation, to a person, to a place, etc... Fear teaches us where we find ourselves mentally at any given moment.

We must not deny the toxic fear, we must feel it and act in spite of it, following the "internal GPS" we have for our emotions (more about this GPS will be explained later). The masters understand that fear as an emotion is very useful in indicating where we are, where we are stuck in our personal growth process. Behind that fear lies our true potential, our essence. That is why if you walk toward your fears you obtain freedom. Doing the opposite imprisons you and puts limits on you.

Often, by avoiding our fears and not facing up to them, we sacrifice things that we like, our potential, the chance to live a full life.

Fear is an illusion made larger by the ego and as such it contributes to feelings of resistance, anger and powerlessness.

Imaginary or toxic fear tries to ensure that you never make mistakes and that you adapt to your limiting mental codes, which are our dysfunctional beliefs.

The appearance of fear is an unequivocal sign that indicates our degree of connection with life or with the present moment.

When we worry, or feel preoccupied by something, we are feeling fear instead of dealing with the situation. As an example, take the word "preoccupy". If we divide it we have the prefix "pre" (meaning before) and the verb "occupy"; that is, being concerned about something before its time.

If we live in the present, allowing things to be as they are, engaging with every instant, we will live completely without fear.

Many Tibetan lamas say that fear is the natural response of your mind when you get close to the truth, and the truth is discovering who you really are.

What do the masters do?

They allow themselves to feel the fear with acceptance, without repressing or hiding it.

They acknowledge it and become familiar with it, understanding that, in one way or another, its function is protection. They simply say thank you to it and "dance" with it towards their objective, or in the direction that life is inviting them to flow. They understand that the true antidote to feeling afraid is, precisely, to do what we fear.

They take it as a challenge that will help them obtain the best possible version of themselves (connecting with their essence or true self).

They ask themselves what wisdom is behind the fear.

The first thing they do is acknowledge it, accept it, look at it with perspective and, once it has been accepted, ask themselves whether it is biological or imaginary.

Questions such as "can this action, which it seems I am afraid of, cause my life to end or cause a fatal illness?" are the ones they use to determine whether it is a biological fear or a psychological fear. If the response to this question is yes, they know they are dealing with a biological fear the purpose of which is to protect us from a real danger. However, if the answer is no, they understand that it is only a limiting fear that they can overcome simply by "dancing" with it, moving towards their objective despite the fear.

They remind us that resigning ourselves to a fear that has us paralyzed and limited is like kissing the hand of the murderer who is strangling us, taking our life away from us.

What do the masters not do?

They do not run from fear.

They do not consider it real: they believe it is a false projection of the conceptual mind or conflict-oriented mindset.

They do not resist it, they do not fight it and they do not use it as an excuse behind which to hide. They do not sacrifice their life, or their internal power, because of it.

They do not give up, they do not allow themselves to be trapped by it. They do not struggle against it.

They do not ignore it or repress it.

I have an anecdote about this, something funny that happened a few months ago. During a conference I attended somebody commented that the only people who are not afraid are idiots. This reminded me that my Tibetan name is Karma Jikme Dorje, which means "he who has no fear" or, in this case, "the big idiot".

In short, at a level we can comprehend, we all feel fear: the thing is not to deny that fear, but rather to act in spite of it.

Practice:

Seated in your favorite meditation position, take at least three deep breaths and observe and accept how you feel, without resistance:

Then make the following affirmations, with a sense of connection to your inner feelings:

"I am letting go of everything false that disconnects me from life. Those projections are not me, they are not real".

Focus your attention on your heart, on the spot that separates the two halves of your ribcage, for several minutes or longer.

Think about a situation that really makes you afraid and allow yourself to feel the emotion.

As you inhale, feel, at the mental and emotional levels, how you lovingly take that fear and tell it, since somehow its function was to protect you:

"Thank you, but you are no longer necessary".

As you exhale, visualize yourself putting it in a small imaginary box in front of you, it doesn't matter at what height. While you are projecting it into the box, you tell it:

I love you.

Repeat this operation until you feel that the box is completely full. Then visualize or feel that the box is slowly moving away from you. It is moving towards the sun and, when it gets there, it melts into it.

Before you finish, connect with your heart for a few minutes and make the following affirmation:

"Thank you, thank you, thank you".

Finally, be grateful for this new day and hope that this meditation will be of benefit to all beings without exception.

Story:

—Excuse me —said one fish to another— You are older than I am and have more experience than I do, so I'm hoping you will be able to help me. Please, tell me, where can I find that thing they call the ocean? I have been looking all over for it, but have had no luck!

—The ocean —said the old fish— is where you are right now.

—This? But this is just water! What I am looking for is the ocean! —replied the younger fish with great disappointment, as he swam away to look somewhere else.

Chapter 4: Gratitude

"Feeling gratitude and not expressing it is like wrapping a present and not giving it".

William Arthur Ward

"Gratitude is the fairest blossom which springs from the soul".

Henry W. Beecher

I have lovely memories of the fascinating trips I made to Bangladesh when I worked for an airline. It always surprised me that a country so full of life and beautiful energy could have so many pockets of extreme poverty.

I still remember a day when I was walking down the street with some co-workers. A group of seven or eight kids were following us. In my pocket I had a piece of sugar free candy that I decided to toss into the air. What happened afterwards will be etched in my heart forever.

A beautiful little girl with her hair in adorable braids, who was about five years old, jumped up high, flying through the air to catch the piece of candy with a big smile on her face. She had barely landed from that gigantic leap when about fifteen kids rushed up all around her.

Worried by what I saw, I went to where they were and gently separated the kids one by one until I reached the little girl, whom I lifted in my arms. When I had her at face level, I asked if she was okay. She quickly put the candy in her mouth, wrapper and all, and smiled. A few seconds later, after spitting out the plastic she had in her mouth, she said:

—Thank you.

I put her back on the ground and left her there laughing and playing with about twenty other children.

A few months later work took me back to the same city. This time I connected in a special way with another of the airline's employees, a young man who had grabbed my attention even before we boarded the plane. He had a big smile and eyes that seemed to emanate light. It was as if his whole being spread optimism, and he managed to raise the spirits of anybody he came across. Sami was his name.

During his breaks, Sami sometimes took an old, time-worn photo out of his wallet and looked at it closely, while his eyes shined with great intensity. On one of these occasions I noticed two tears rolling down his cheeks, so I went up to him, I touched his head gently and asked him if everything was alright. He looked at me intensely and responded:

—José, my friend, I don't know why but I feel a very good connection with you, so I am going to tell you something that I haven't shared with any other co-workers up to now.

Then he showed me a photo of four beautiful children, sitting in order of age: the youngest was a baby aged about one year and the oldest looked to be no more than four. They were so lovely, with their eyes shining brightly, as if someone on the other side of the camera was making funny faces at them! These adorable creatures had dark skin and their enormous eyes stood out on their spirited faces. They looked like little dolls, and it made you want to give them a big hug.

—These were my brothers and sisters. —They *were* or they *are?* ❧

—Well... —responded Sami after a pause— You see José, my parents were very poor, so poor that they couldn't feed all of us. They had to gradually stop feeding two of us so that the other two could survive. Otherwise, all four of us would have died. Soon, two of my siblings got sick and died. They chose us randomly. I am the third and my brother is the second. Since my parents told me this story, when I was still young, I am thankful to life for giving me this opportunity.

Sami paused for a moment to take a breath and then, with great emotion, he said:

—Every day when I wake up, I give thanks for everything. My first thought is for my siblings: I don't want their death to be in vain so I try to make sure my life brings meaning and value to the world; that is why

I live with passion, joy and enthusiasm. That is what I would want my siblings to do if it had been me that had died.

When I heard this I was speechless. What an incredible lesson about life I was receiving from this young man! All the worries floating around in my head disappeared in an instant. My eyes suddenly opened to the fact that this kind of thing and situation really do occur. Like an old Sufi saying: "I cursed the fact that I had no shoes until I saw a man who had no feet".

According to an "ordinary" mentality, that young man had every reason in the world to curse his luck, to live with the belief that life is cruel and unfair, to blame others for his situation. However, he had decided to focus on the positive aspects of his experience: he was still alive and he did not want the death of his siblings to have been in vain, so he decided he had to give meaning to it all. Every day he was grateful for the opportunity to keep on living and to continue giving beautiful things to the world, encouraging and motivating all the people around him. He decided not to play the role of victim, but rather to take the path of the courageous!

As Helen Keller said: "No pessimist ever discovered the secret of the stars or sailed to an uncharted land, or opened a new doorway for the human spirit".

What do the masters say?

In this life there are two paths before us at all times: that of love or that of fear. The latter is considered by the masters to be false or illusory, a path mined with suffering.

If you take the path of love, any situation will be an opportunity to grow, to evolve, to learn... If you take the other path, you are choosing a victim mentality, complaints, powerlessness and self-generated drama. We are constantly making decisions of this type.

Living in gratitude and appreciation is the highest option you can choose. It connects you with the highest vibrations of life, with health, well-being, understanding, peace and happiness.

When you are grateful, says Kalu T., you open the door to everyday miracles, and the best miracle of all occurs when you realize that your true nature is love.

Living in gratitude is the best way to live life. If we are grateful, our minds and bodies expand. Emotionally, we feel lighter and more complete.

When you feel gratitude, everything heals because this is the language of life and of your inner self.

Masters are thankful for everything, even for those situations that an "ordinary" person would consider totally undesirable. They are thankful for them because they understand that life is giving them that situation so that they will remember their true nature, and show the best version of themselves. As the saying goes, pressure is what turns carbon into a diamond.

What do the masters do?

They constantly feel gratitude for everything, without exception: their life, their health, the lessons they learn...

They choose to take everything as a chance to grow, so they are grateful for each opportunity that life offers them.

They live in constant appreciation, because gratitude has the same frequency as love and love is the essence of life.

They feel grateful even to those beings that others might consider unpleasant, because they see them as "mirrors" that show what they can correct within themselves.

One of their mantras is the following: Thank you, thank you, thank you! They are always sharing their joy.

They motivate all beings without exception (with actions or with words).

They practice daily gratitude: when you feel gratitude, everything heals because this is the language of life and of your inner self.

What do the masters not do?

They do not curse their situation or their luck. They do not complain.

They do not build an identity out of their story of pain or suffering.

They do not let any situation go by without feeling grateful for it. They do not resist.

They do not focus on being victims.

They do not curse what happens to them.

They do not make suffering real by identifying with what are apparently painful situations.

Practice:

Connect with your heart and spend a few minutes, or the amount of time you think is right, feeling grateful for everything in your life that contributes to your well-being.

Feel grateful for the things in your life that you do not like, thanking them for giving you the opportunity to grow and show the best version of yourself.

Finally, hope that this meditation will be of benefit to all beings without exception.

Do this practice every day for 21 days and observe, consciously and without expectations, the changes that start to occur in your life.

Story:

There is a story about a man who was driving through the desert when his car got a flat tire. When he stepped out of the car to change the tire, he discovered he had no jack. Fortunately, he remembered having passed a house that seemed to be inhabited just a few kilometers back. He decided to walk to the house and ask whoever was there if they could loan him a jack. It was already getting dark and as he walked our friend started to think:

—Will they open the door for me? What if they don't? What if someone opens the door but is angry with me for getting him out of bed because tomorrow he has to get up early? What if he doesn't have a jack? What if he has one but doesn't want to loan it to me? As he got closer and closer to the house, his thoughts became increasingly turbulent. He got so worked up that when he reached the house and rang the doorbell, all he could do when they opened the door was to shout:

—*You can take your damned jack and stuff it where the sun doesn't shine!*

Chapter 5: Not making assumptions

"Wisdom is learning what to overlook".

William James

"An untrained mind is an open door to suffering".

Master Kalu. T

I am going to share something that had a big impact on me. When I was working abroad at an airline, I had a good friend with whom I shared great times and great conversations. He was Spanish and his name was Toni.

My friend Toni was a wonderful guy. However, he seemed to have some insecurities that were especially bad in the area of love and relationships. They had grown worse after his two most recent relationships with women, which had failed miserably. In Tony's view, they had failed because of these women's inability to understand him. But things seemed to be changing: he had met Laura, one of the loveliest women at the airline.

Laura was the closest thing to an angel I had ever seen: light brown hair, blue eyes shining with happiness and enthusiasm, a sweet voice always filled with love and respect. It was one of those people who brought a smile on your face every time you think about her. It seems that destiny had brought my friend Toni's and Laura's paths together during a "Spanish dinner" organized by some mutual friends. They connected with each other marvelously and, as we tend to say in these cases, "Cupid" made his appearance and a lovely romance began. About four months into the relationship, the following occurred:

Laura's old boyfriend, Mark, had left the company suddenly because he had to return to Australia to deal with family matters. So he and Laura had not seen each other since their break-up, seven or eight months ago. Toni knew that on April 7th, *Mark the Australian*, would be back in the country, so, early in the day, he called his girlfriend to find out what was happening. She did not respond to that first call, or to the ten calls that came after it in the space of two hours, time that our friend Toni spent checking and rechecking the flight schedule of the airline in which Mark was travelling. As the hours passed, he asked himself where Laura could be and why she would not answer his calls. The worst thing was not that he asked himself these questions, but rather that he started answering them himself, coming up with an entire conspiracy theory that proved what he already suspected: that all women are bad (bad was not quite the word that came out of his mouth) and will betray you the first chance they get. And he told his girlfriend exactly what he was thinking in at least 20 messages, the intensity of which rose *in crescendo*, and which he left for all of posterity on both Laura's cell phone and her landline.

That very day, April 7th, about twenty-five of us had been invited to Toni's apartment at 7 p.m. for a surprise birthday party. When the door opened, we all shouted:

—Happy birthday Toni!

My friend practically went into shock. He had had no idea whatsoever. He started hugging everyone there, thanking them for the big surprise; but at the same time, his heart racing, he was trying, without success, to find his beloved Laura in the crowd. When he gave up looking, he asked what had been torturing him all day long:

—Well now, where is Laura?

Her best friend was the one who answered:

—I don't know... She arrived bright and early and spent all day getting things ready for the party, but then in the afternoon she called to say she didn't feel well, that we should have a good time without her, and that she would be in touch with you.

Toni's face was as expressive as a poem, but the poem came from a horror story. I had never seen such an unhappy birthday boy. In a matter of hours, his mental and emotional toxicity had destroyed a great relationship and done serious harm to the person who had put her heart into throwing that surprise party. A person who had probably not answered his calls because she suspected the emotion and nerves in her voice would give away the surprise. The reason that Laura did not pick up the phone was not that she was deceiving him but quite the opposite: she was incapable of lying.

After all of those insults, Laura wanted to have nothing to do with my friend and naturally the relationship ended. When that night a terribly dejected Toni told me what had happened, I encouraged him simply to ask himself a question: "What is the lesson to be learned from all this?" He understood the lesson and absorbed it.

Whenever you speak, make sure that your words are connected to love and that they are, at the very least, better than silence. Communicate with others; do not make assumptions. Do not poison the people around you or your relationships with lethal conjectures and all the emotional toxicity that they tend to carry with them. Express yourself from a place of affection and comprehension.

What do the masters say?

Assumptions are the preferred weapon of the conflict-oriented mindset. Their venom is as lethal as the most poisonous snake. They can create absolutely surreal stories, genuine tales of horror, if we give them free rein and actually believe them.

When you make an assumption, you impose your memory of the past on the present and use it as a guide, and as a reference, you are using false and conflictive conjectures. This causes suffering.

We see the world according to what we are: so, if we are afraid and full of insecurity, we will make assumptions based on fears, superstitions, judgments and attacks.

The reactionary mind thinks it needs to know everything and if it cannot, it will invent stories to feed its assumptions.

When we assume something, we are distorting reality and seeing something false, something that our conceptual mind creates based on bad past experiences, frustrations and fears, in order to relive the memory and emotion as conditioned by our mind.

The masters recommend that we empty everything of meaning so that we are able to uncover the truth concealed beneath our beliefs, ideas and suppositions. To do so, they advise us to apply a powerful mantra, infallible when it comes to putting a brake on those toxic mental processes: "I don't know!"

According to all of my teachers, questioning the reactionary or conceptual mind (which is explained in depth in Chapter 30) is the way to start connecting with your true nature, which is peace, and also to gain access to universal wisdom; for this reason, for ages, many teachers have instructed their students to constantly question this mentality that needs to know everything, by saying "I don't know" or "None of this means what I think it does". Even Socrates himself stated: "I only know that I know nothing..." And curiously enough he went down in history as one of the wisest of the wise.

As an example, I would like to share the following text, which comes from a personal blog written by Ibán Bermúdez Betancor, a student and ex-patient of mind that cured himself of cancer in 7 months, complementing his medical treatments with the practices that I teach in my courses and are described in this book.

"Three tools have taught me to separate myself from those thoughts that confuse us and trap us; if we were to apply a big "I don't know" or "my thoughts mean absolutely nothing" or "this situation does not mean what I think it does" each time that a thought infects us with its fear, we would create space as we make them disappear, an empty space that we could fill with peace".

(You will find Ibán's complete text at the end of the book).

What do the masters do?

When they see the assumption coming, they make a conscious response that immediately puts a stop to the process:
—I don't know!
—I don't have the answer.

—None of this means what I think it does. —I love you.

If they have any questions, they ask.

They communicate with the person instead of assuming things. They observe without making judgments, they allow things to be as they are.

What do the masters not do?

They do not allow themselves to be dragged down by the kinds of thoughts that believe they know or should know everything.

They do not interpret.

They do not add or impose a story to what is happening, they allow things to be as they are. They do not guess.

They do not make up stories.

They do not take things for granted.

They do not allow their thoughts to disconnect them from the present. They do not judge or condemn.

They do not make conclusions regarding things that have not yet occurred.

Practice:

When thoughts related to assumptions come into your "head," take three deep breaths and repeat:

"I am letting go of everything false that disconnects me from life. Those projections are not me, they are not real, because I am peace".

Focus your attention on your heart, on the spot between the two halves of your ribcage, for a few minutes or longer.

And affectionately tell those thoughts:

"I don't know! I choose peace".

Finally, hope that the benefits of this meditation will reach all beings without exception.

Story:

The Master would often say that one of the reasons people are so unhappy is they think there is nothing that they cannot change.

He especially liked the story of the person who was talking to a radio salesman:

—This transistor radio you sold me sounds excellent, but I would like to exchange it for one that has better programs.

Anthony de Mello

Chapter 6: Responsibility

"The greatest gift you have to give is that of your own self-transformation."

Lao Tse

"If every one of us would sweep our own doorstep, the whole world would be clean".

Mother Teresa of Calcutta

I have a nephew named David who used to love to run down the hall like a madman at my parents' house. The little guy moved like a rocket and reached incredible speeds but his "braking system" was not terribly effective and he ended up colliding into the same corner time after time. After the usual accident, the same situation always occurred: my sister picked up the crying child and, with the best of intentions, she tried to console him by saying:

—Did the wall give you a boo-boo? Come here, let's give that bad wall a kick.

On one of these occasions, while a tearful David was kicking the wall, wiping his eyes and saying "bad wall," I went up to him and asked:

—David, how old are you?

—Four —he said proudly holding up four fingers.

—Ok. Now, do you know how many years this wall has been in the same place? —I repeated the question while he looked at me in perplexity, not understanding what I was trying to get at—. Twenty years. So, do you really think that it's the wall's fault that you always run into it?

First he scratched his head, then he smiled and finally he said:

—No.

My nephew took in this great lesson in responsibility quite admirably. But not long afterwards, he again fell down in that fateful spot. When she heard the fall, my sister rushed to help him while saying:

—That darn wall again! Let's give it a good kick!

The boy rushed forward and stood between my sister and the corner:

—No, mama! It was me. It's not the wall's fault —he said quickly.

—Oh, I see! It looks like you have been talking with your uncle José... —my sister said with a smile on her face.

I also smiled, glad to know that my nephew was no longer weaving in his mind the always distasteful role of victim.

Months later something very sweet took place. We were walking down a street in Arrecife (on the island of Lanzarote) when my nephew let go of my hand and ran towards a construction worker who was using a power drill to tear down the corner of an old house. The worker turned around when he felt someone pulling on his shirt and there was a blond-haired, blue-eyed little boy looking at him sternly. Surprised, he turned off the machine and took off his ear protection to listen to what the little boy had to say:

—Hey you, don't break the wall! Can't you see it's not the wall's fault? —admonished the child.

This left the man speechless so I went up to him and told him the whole story. The man laughed and soothed my nephew, telling him not to worry, that he would keep in mind what David had said. My nephew, much calmer now, and I continued along our way.

What do the masters say?

From a very young age, our parents, family and environment induce us to adopt the kind of attitude that blames others instead of assuming responsibility. For many, it turns into a habit. As a result we go through the world "running into walls" in the different realms of our lives: health, relationships, work... There is always somebody else to blame! So we concentrate on cursing those "walls" and trying to tear them down,

44

or we spend all our time complaining and criticizing the walls we believe to be the cause of our discomfort or unhappiness, refusing to take responsibility for our lives.

We constantly hear expressions like these, which reveal a victim mentality:

—It's my husband's, wife's, boyfriend's, girlfriend's fault...

—The government, or politicians, are to blame...

—It's because my boss, or my co-workers...

Feeling that you are a victim puts you squarely in a conflict-oriented mindset or in a reactionary mind (ego), which causes you to limit yourself, to judge yourself and to feel that you are powerless. We must wake up from this lie or mental virus that takes away the power we have inside us. A sense of responsibility is the antidote needed, because it helps us to connect with who we really are. We must realize that we can decide to perceive things differently, choosing love as our teacher.

To do so, these teachers use forgiveness, releasing others from fault, because they know that everything in their reality is a projection of themselves.

They take responsibility, which means being aware that the power is inside them; at the very moment they take responsibility, things start to change. They leave behind the powerlessness associated with the "victim of the circumstances" role, to live their lives and their own reality intensely.

What do the masters do?

They assume their responsibility and they undertake actions that are connected to life, feeling inspired to find the best solution.

They understand that nothing can hurt you without your consent. They release others from guilt by forgiving.

They know they are creators, that they have the same power as the Universe. Therefore, they create their own reality with the only mind possible: an innocent or unitary mind (free of judgment) which is what connects with all of life's potential. One of the great teachers, Jesus, said this:

—"Let the children come to me. Don't stop them! For the Kingdom of Heaven belongs to those who are like these children". They connect with their internal power in all circumstances.

What do the masters not do?

They never blame others.
They never under any circumstances take the role of victim.
They do not stop living at their maximum potential, even in situations that the ordinary mind would consider harsh.
They do not curse the darkness; instead, they light a candle.
They do not miss any opportunity that life gives them to continue discovering their true nature.

Practice:

Think of some person or situation that you tend to think is "to blame" for your unhappiness. Why does it cause discomfort in you?
Now repeat, feeling the power of these affirmations:

"I forgive myself for judging you".
"I free you of my judgment, of thinking that you are the cause of my suffering". "I take responsibility: you are innocent, I am innocent".
"I understand that all situations are there for me to discover who I really am (and my internal power)".
"I understand that everyone acts according to his or her level of consciousness, and that level is frequently ignorance".
"I love you. I love myself".

Finally, hope that the benefits of this meditation will reach all beings without exception.

Story:

There is a story about a man who accidentally fell off a cliff, but he was lucky enough that halfway down he was able to grab hold of a shrub that was sticking out of the cliff face and thus avoid, temporarily, the tremendous crash to the ground.

—Help! Please help! —The man shouted over and over again, in desperation—. Is there anybody out there who can help me?

Suddenly the clouds opened up and a thunderous voice was heard:

—My son, this is God speaking. You have begged for help so much that I have taken mercy on you. Let go, let yourself fall and before you hit the ground I will have sent two angels who will kindly catch you and place you gently on the ground.

The man was silent for a few seconds and then he shouted again with all his might:

—Help! Help! Is there anybody else out there who can help me?

Chapter 7:
Placing your trust in life and the Universe

"You don't have enough faith", Jesus told them. "I tell you the truth, if you had faith even as small as a mustard seed, you could say to this mountain, 'Move from here to there,' and it would move. Nothing would be impossible

Mathew 17:20

"In the middle of difficulty lies opportunity".

Albert Einstein

There was still over a week before the end of the month and, that Monday, there was only one thing emptier than my bank account: my refrigerator. Ten Euros, two apples and one egg made up my entire arsenal for survival until my next paycheck arrived.

Many of you are probably asking yourselves how in the world I had gotten myself into such a situation. As it happened, I was conscious of the fact that, at a moment of great emotion and inspiration, I had invested all my money for that month in my great passion: painting. And that Monday I knew I had to prioritize and invest my last ten Euros correctly. So I got dressed, I went to the shop and gave my last ten Euros to the cashier, in exchange for a can of red acrylic paint that I urgently needed to finish some paintings I had been working on for the past several days.

I stayed up late painting, enjoying myself immensely. Not long before, I had learned from a master of Japanese painting something that fascinated me and that since then I have done in all of my works: before painting the picture, I write a few small blessings or good wishes on the canvas, so that wherever the painting ends up it will fill the people around it with light, health and happiness.

Around four in the morning I looked at the paintings, definitely the best work I had ever done, and went to bed. My stomach was empty but my heart was full. The next morning, still half-asleep, I went to the kitchen, opened the refrigerator, and confirmed that the bread and fish miracle did not work with apples and eggs. I smiled and said to myself: "Relax, the Universe will take care of things".

Really, I was truly calm and convinced that this would be the case. I had learned this from my teachers: these great masters had shown me how to simply allow life *to be*, how to enjoy life like a child.

Later, in the afternoon, while, brush in hand, I was touching up a few details, the doorbell rang. It turned out to be an old friend and fellow-surfer whom I hadn't seen for a long time. He had heard that I painted and wanted to see my paintings.

From the very beginning there was one in particular that grabbed his attention. He found it fascinating because it reminded him of a very intense experience he had had years ago, in his early years as a surfer. His eyes gleamed as he looked at it, as he examined each detail, and he could not stop trying to describe the intensity of the feelings that the painting created in him.

After about an hour, he asked me the price of the painting. I explained that it was a key element in an exhibition that I was preparing but he insisted that I give him a figure, so I told him it cost about nine hundred Euros. With great sadness he said he thought that was a fair price but that unfortunately he could not afford it... He didn't even have enough money to fill up his gas tank!

He looked one last time at the painting, like someone who is saying goodbye to a loved one and wants to remember every last detail, and he went toward the door.

—Alex, I have an idea. Today I haven't got anything to eat, so I will exchange the painting for a sandwich —I told him.

It took me awhile to convince him that I wasn't joking and finally he decided to accept my offer:

—José, not just a sandwich... I'll get you a side of potatoes and any kind of juice you want!

So, there we were, my friend Alex, the painting (which he wouldn't let out of his sight) and I, in a small café not far away. I will never forget the sandwich of fried squid, the plate of potatoes and the peach juice that I savored as if they were the most exquisite delicacies on earth, while my friend talked non-stop about everything the painting transmitted to him.

I looked at him and thought how fantastic it is to be able to make people happy. I remembered an old Tibetan saying in which a student says to his teacher:

—Master, I am sad. What can I do? —Go out and make someone happy —answers the teacher.

We said goodbye after several hours of interesting conversation, and he disappeared with the painting in his arms.

When I got home, I laid down on the bed and, while listening to the sound of the sea in the background, I thought: "Fantastic! Today I have eaten and I have thoroughly enjoyed myself. I am satisfied. Tomorrow will also be a great day". And I fell asleep feeling deeply grateful for all the blessings I had in my life.

The next day, when I woke up, I was surprised to see that I had fifteen missed calls from Alex. I quickly listened to the five voice messages that my friend had left.

—Hey buddy, how are you? I showed your painting to my uncle, who is here on vacation. Tomorrow he returns to Germany but before he leaves he wants to see more of your paintings. Can we drop by your house later this morning?

I returned his calls and within two hours Alex was at my house with his uncle Hans, who seemed very happy since, he said, the blue tones in my work really resonated with him. He decided to buy four paintings, which solved all my financial woes not just for that month but also for the next two months.

What could I say? When he left, I simply looked at the sky, thanked the Universe and smiled.

Always have trust, not just at the mental level, but with the whole of your inner self, and connected with how you feel. You will notice a big difference in your life.

What do the masters say?

When you place your trust in life and the Universe, the Universe will return that trust to you with blessings. When you do what you love, the Universe responds by showing you that you are on the right path. Similarly, if you resign yourself to doing something you don't love, life will show you, through your inner feelings, that this is not your path.

Creativity is the language of the soul, or of your essence. Therefore, whenever you are creative, you are totally connected with the Universal energy.

The Universe does not understand words, it only understands the language of feelings and, if you really feel trust and you love what you do, the Universe will connect with your inner feelings and will help you manifest what is in your heart.

What do the masters do?

They do whatever it is that they love.

They enjoy every moment without worrying about tomorrow. They align with life through faith and joy.

They trust fully in life.

They share with others without expecting anything in return. They accept everything as it is.

They allow themselves to express their creativity because that is the expression of the spirit.

Whatever happens, they always feel content.

What do the masters not do?

They do not feel mistrust.

They do not force things to be a certain way.

They do not leave the path because of fear.

They do not resign themselves, out of fear or laziness, to a life they do not love. They do not lose hope.

They do not look for happiness outside of themselves.

Practice:

While connecting with your feelings, ask the Universe (or Life, or God, or whatever you wish to call it) the following:

"I give myself to you with total trust, joy and humility so that you may guide me and help me connect with or develop some talent or activity that can serve others, can help make the world a better place and, especially, enable me remember who I really am, for the benefit all beings without exception".

And then say:

"Thank you, thank you, thank you".

Finally, express your hope that the benefits of this meditation will reach all beings without exception.

Story:

The monastery was becoming too small and a larger building had to be built. So a businessman wrote a check for one million dollars and put it down in front of the master, who picked it up and said:

—Excellent! I'll take it.

The businessman felt disappointed: he had donated an enormous amount of money and the master had not even said thank you!

—That check is worth a million dollars —he said.

—Yes, I realize that —responded the wise teacher.

—Although I am a very rich man, a million dollars is a lot of money —continued the businessman.

—Yes, it is. Would you like to thank me? —inquired the master.

—It is you who should be thanking me! —replied the businessman in surprise.

—Me? Why me? It is he who gives who must be grateful —said the teacher.

Chapter 8: Expecting nothing in return

"If one does not understand a person,
one tends to regard him as a fool".

Carl G. Jung

"In this life there is no suffering or joy, just changes.
Depending on your degree of resistance to such changes,
you will experience one thing or the other".

Mr. Díaz

The first rays of sun were just beginning to light up the sky. Javi (that is what I will call him to protect his identity) and I were especially happy because the evening before the weather report had predicted large waves that day in the northern part of the island.

Javi was (and still is) a great surfer, well known for his strength, skill and courage. We could say that he seemed to meet all the requirements for being considered one of those "tough guys," which made him quite well respected (and even feared) by both local and foreign surfers in the western part of the island.

At seven in the morning, it was just me and him in the water, enjoying some big waves that were beautiful, powerful and fast-moving. My friend had not slept well the night before: I could see he had less concentration and balance than he usually had. I imagined it had something to do with the rough patch he was going through in his relationship, so I decided not to make a big deal of it, although I tried to keep an eye on him just in case any complications arose.

As the tide rose, the intensity of the waves increased. All of a sudden, I saw a series of three or four gigantic ones right next to my friend, crashing over him and putting him into a very difficult situation.

After the first wave, and for a few seconds that seemed like ages, I could not see my friend in the white foam and turbulent water, so I headed over as fast as I could while shouting his name. I saw his board bouncing at the mercy of the waves and the broken tether, an indication of nothing good. To make matters worse, I could see the next series not far off and coming towards us at a fast pace. In the brief space of time before the next series, I had a glimpse of my friend's body, floating face down.

I knew I had to get there before the next impact, because, being unconscious, he ran the risk of being thrown against the rocks by the huge masses of water that were approaching so threateningly. I rowed with all my might and managed to grab hold of him just seconds before the first wave hit us. I thought I felt my bones crack as we were hit by the second. I managed to go under water, holding on to my friend, to avoid the third wave, which looked like the worst of all. My board also got away from me, and I shivered when I saw it fall to pieces, literally, against the rocks.

I made it to the shore of volcanic rocks, but the current was so strong that it was hard to lift myself out of the water, and we ended up being tossed mercilessly back and forth. In one of the sea's violent thrusts, in an attempt to protect my friend from a blow that probably would have killed him, I put my shoulder between his head and the sharp volcanic rocks. I felt my wetsuit rip, taking part of my skin with it. I felt blood flowing down my back but, because of the tension of the moment, I felt no pain.

Although to this day I don't know how I did it, I managed to get my friend out of the water and I confirmed that he was not breathing. I quickly laid him face-up on the ground and started doing mouth-to-mouth resuscitation. Soon he started coughing and spitting up water. He was in a state of shock for a few minutes, trying to assimilate the situation. Then the strangest thing happened. He pushed me away roughly, sat up and, looking at me with eyes full of rage, he said in a challenging tone:

—Don't say anything about this to anybody!

He stood up in fury, went to get his board, grabbed his clothes and sped off in his car.

I sat there in confusion: I was dazed and disoriented, I couldn't understand what had happened, and furthermore I was beginning to feel the pain of my injured back. In the background, a curious "soundtrack" could be heard: the sounds made by my surfboard (or what was left of it, I should say) as it bounced to and fro, crashing against the rocks, like pieces of a broken toy.

I decided to put into practice what my teachers had taught me. They had shown me the importance of acting without expecting anything in return and of always asking myself, no matter how incomprehensible, harsh or unbelievable the situation might seem, what it was that I could learn from it. So that is what I did. I looked inside and said to myself:

—What is the opportunity here?

Then I smiled and decided to simply feel glad that my friend was still alive.

When thoughts about why my friend had reacted that way came into my mind, I applied the infallible mantra that my teachers had taught me: "I don't know!" And that way I felt peace and full acceptance of everything that had occurred.

As the weeks passed, I noticed that Javi avoided me and did not return my calls; the only thing I did was accept it, leave him his space and send him love and the benefits of some of my meditations.

Two years later we happened to see each other at an event. I went up to him, smiled and said:

—I'm sorry if that day there was something that bothered you. I only did what any friend would do for another.

Javi looked at me and could not hold back the tears. He gave me such a big hug that my ribs hurt and he said:

—I'm the one who should apologize; I didn't do a good job handling my anger.

He explained to me that he had acted the way he did because he feared that his reputation as a great surfer, one highly respected by all, would be damaged. He also confessed that he felt frustrated when he saw that his weakness had become visible and he had to be rescued by someone else, in this case, an amateur surfer like me, a witness and constant reminder that one day he had failed.

At the end of the conversation we agreed that we were grateful for everything that had occurred and we said goodbye with a big hug.

It was a lovely encounter. Now, years later, whenever I have a little free time and want to get away from it all, Javi is there to go surfing with me.

What do the masters say?

When you do something for someone, do not hope to get something in return: do not do it for the recognition, the gratitude, or the honor it might bring you. Do it simply because love motivates you to do it.

The expectations we have in relation to our actions can frustrate and disappoint us if the results we expected do not come about. Expectations that people will react in a certain way are programmed into us and if things do not turn out the way we expect, we enter a state of resistance and suffering.

There are people who have a particular image of themselves or the type of personality that, in situations that reveal their vulnerability, leads them to react violently to the help offered to them, since their conflict-oriented mindset or their ego is especially disturbed at that time. The ego, or the conflict-oriented mindset, acts as a filter that distorts people's perception of the facts, and so, even in a situation in which someone has saved their life, they may become angry and lash out.

What do the masters do?

They engage in acts motivated by unconditional love and emotion, without expecting or hoping for anything in return.

They always feel gratitude to life and all beings, but they do not expect anybody to thank them or appreciate their actions.

They understand that people are not really free when they live with and identify with reactionary, mental programs that disconnect them from love; therefore, the masters always apply compassion to those beings. In Tibetan Buddhism, the meaning of the word "compassion" is "to help others stop suffering". This differs considerably from how the word is conceived in the West, where it is associated with pity, a concept that reinforces and promulgates the role of victim and powerlessness.

What do the masters not do?

They have no expectations.
They do not expect recognition for their actions. They do not expect to receive gratitude.
They do not have a personal motive that makes them want to help. They do not interpret.
They do not judge the reactionary
behavior of people who live in ignorance.
They do not act out of personal interest.

Practice:

At any time during the day, when you find yourself in a situation in which someone needs help, do something for that person and do it with an attitude of non-expectation, without trying to obtain that person's gratitude in exchange. And observe the beautiful feeling that envelopes you.

Story:

Two Tibetan monks saw each other after spending several years in prison, where they had suffered unspeakable torture at the hands of their prisoners.

—Have you forgiven them? —asked the first monk.

—I will never forgive them! Never! —responded the second.

—Well then, —said the first—, in that case, it would seem that you are still imprisoned, aren't you?

Buddhist proverb

Chapter 9: Forgiveness

"To understand everything is to forgive everything".

Buddha

"If you do not forgive for love, forgive at least for selfishness, for your own welfare".

Dalai Lama

"Do not judge, and you will not be judged.
Do not condemn, and you will not be condemned".

Saint Luke 6, 36-38

In the 1950s, during the Chinese invasion of Tibet, this country's population was decimated: in Lhasa alone about ninety thousand people perished. The innumerable acts of war, my teachers have told me, included the destruction of dozens of temples, and along with them, the disappearance of huge amounts of spiritual information of great value, and of many other elements that this culture holds sacred. Many people know about the dramatic situation faced by those forced to flee Tibet, among them the Dalai Lama himself, who took refuge in Dharamsala, in northern India.

Many of the Tibetan teachers I have met over the years have shared with me what that escape was like. However, the story that had the greatest impact on me was that of a teacher we will call Khempo.

Khempo was only ten when a group of soldiers burst into his house. In cold blood, with a shot in the head, they murdered his mother, his father and his sister. They forced him to watch the killings and then they let him go. This was a practice they repeated with many other families.

The idea behind it was to traumatize an entire generation; a generation that would live their whole life in a state of fear and anguish.

When disconsolate Khempo, in a state of terror and exhaustion, finally reached the border with the help of his uncle, he broke into tears and, looking at his only surviving family member, he exclaimed:

—What are we going to do now? We have lost everything!

—No, dear nephew, we are still alive —responded his uncle.

That was the great motivation that led little Khempo to keep going and to be grateful for every day.

During his lifetime, Khempo had many panic attacks and nightmares but he worked through these issues with the help of meditation and Tibetan Buddhist philosophy. He made so much progress that he ended up becoming a teacher specialized in transcending fear. He made use of his painful past to grow spiritually and he eventually became a great lama.

The most impressive part of this story occurred when Khempo was about sixty years old. According to some people who know him, and according to what he himself would confirm to me later, in one of his trips he came across one of the Chinese soldiers that had shot his family. Thanks to the personal development and spiritual evolution of these masters, they are able to recognize people through their essence or energy, and not through their physical appearance. He went up to him and asked him if, fifty years ago, he had shot an entire family in cold blood, turning a ten-year-old child into a defenseless orphan. The soldier started crying. He sobbed and wailed in pain. Khempo gave him a hug and simply said:

—I have already forgiven you and I have forgiven myself. Now you must forgive yourself.

The soldier cried like a child. All he could do was say:

—I'm so sorry, I'm so sorry... Thank you, thank you...

Here we have the greatest act of forgiveness and compassion that the writer of this book has ever heard.

These masters are able to replace such toxic emotions as rancor and the drive for vengeance with compassion. They know that one of the soul's most dangerous poisons is resentment.

For the ego and its thought system (Chapter 30) justice is understood to be some form of vengeance, but for the true inner self, justice is equality.

What do the masters say?

Forgiving frees us from suffering and illness.

Forgiving is the tool with which to acquire a sense of responsibility and internal power, and it is the key to letting go of the role of victim.

Our natural state is peace and love. If we do not forgive, we are going against our own nature, which is total acceptance, love and innocence. Therefore, if we do not forgive, we suffer, as if we were attacking ourselves.

Forgiveness gives us back our innocence. According to all of the great teachers (Jesus, Buddha...), we must act as innocent children if we want to enter the kingdom of heaven, which is nothing but true inner peace. The word innocence comes from the Greek and means "soul free of guilt".

True forgiveness means letting go of the past so that we can be free of its tyranny and the control it has over our lives.

Forgiving does not mean agreeing with what has been done to us, but rather freeing ourselves of toxic emotions such as resentment, bitterness and hate.

What do the masters do?

They are in a state of constant comprehension and appreciation.

They use forgiveness to free themselves of a painful past or of suffering.

They forgive in order to release burdens, to not be weighed down by unnecessary suffering and pain.

They know that there are no bad people or people who perform actions with evil intentions. There are only ignorant people who live under the distorting effect of the reactionary mind, but who, if they had sufficient tools and wisdom, would act differently.

They understand that to hurt others is to hurt oneself.

Many of the teachers I know do not even have to use forgiveness, because they have reached such a high level of consciousness that they do not find offense in anything, in any situation.

They accept fully, letting go of the past that could rob them of the present. They choose being happy instead of being right.

What do the masters not do?

They do not live with rancor, resentment, hate... They do not seek vengeance.

They do not attack those who seem to hurt them.

They do not allow themselves to become sick from such toxic emotions as guilt and hate.

They do not judge, because they know that they themselves would suffer from such punishment.

They do not live burdened by guilt, nor do they constantly search for the guilty parties of the past, because doing so is like trying to put a broken egg back together again. So they let go of the past and say:

—What's done is done and it could not have happened any other way. I acted with the level of consciousness and the tools that I had at that time in my past.

Practice:

Metta Meditation

(Metta is the Tibetan word for "loving kindness")

Seated in your favorite meditation position, focus your attention on your heart and, from that place, make the following affirmations as many times as you wish, feeling the emotion of the words:

"I ask for forgiveness if I have hurt a living being,
whether intentionally or without realizing it".
"I offer my forgiveness to all living beings that have hurt me,
whether intentionally or without realizing it".
"I forgive myself, if I have hurt myself,
whether intentionally or without realizing it".

Finally, express your hope that this meditation will bring benefits to all beings without exception.

Story:

On one occasion Buddha showed a flower to his disciples and asked them to say something about it. They contemplated the flower in silence for awhile.

One disciple gave a philosophical lecture about the flower. Another created a poem. Yet another came up with a parable... They all tried to do better than the others.

Mahakashyapa looked at the flower, smiled and said nothing. Only he had really seen it.

Chapter 10: Tonglen

"Compassion is a far greater and nobler thing than pity. Pity has its roots in fear, and a sense of arrogance and condescension, sometimes even a smug feeling of "I'm glad it's not me." As Stephen Levine says: "When your fear touches someone's pain it becomes pity; when your love touches someone's pain, it becomes compassion." To train in compassion, then, is to know all beings are the same and suffer in similar ways, to honor all those who suffer, and to know you are neither separate from nor superior to anyone".

Sogyal Rinpoche

"All the happiness in the world stems from wanting others to be happy. All the suffering in the world stems from wanting the self to be happy".

Shantideva

When I was little, I often felt out of place: in my family, everything seemed too serious, too limited. I didn't understand why there was so much anger and fear around me. And I didn't see what I had to do with that ambience of upset and vexation: there was something that didn't quite fit, something that bothered me...

I was about eleven when one night, after several days of conflict with my parents and sisters, I went to bed with an immense feeling of sadness. I remember I was lying on the mattress when I started to feel a force growing inside me. I looked at a wooden ironing board that was next to my bed, then I picked up a marker and drew a heart underneath it. I wrote the date and the following words: "I hope I catch all the diseases in the world and that I die instead of them". Afterwards I felt that I was in peace. I fell asleep with a wonderful feeling of disappearing inside and I didn't think about the matter any further.

Ten years later, while I was playing ball with my nephew at my parents' house, the ball rolled into the space just below that ironing board. I went to get it and when I looked up I saw the phrase: "I hope I catch all the diseases in the world and that I die instead of them". I found it very moving, to the point that my eyes filled with tears. Just a few months earlier I had discovered a practice that amazed me and that had a lot to do with the phrase that boy had written long ago under the ironing board. It was Tonglen, the practice of giving and taking.

Tonglen is a method that originated in Tibet two thousand years ago. According to my Tibetan teachers, at the time a leprosy epidemic was decimating the population at an alarming rate. Nobody knew what to do to stop it, until a wise lama gave this tool to the hopeless cases so that they could practice it on each other. By doing so they brought the epidemic to an end.

The first time I used it was with a fellow airline worker whose fingers, for some unknown reason, had seized up. This made it impossible for him to perform his professional duties. The doctors who examined him found no explanation for the problem and he was suffering a great deal. He had been given a medical leave of absence but the company began to talk about letting him go. When I saw how difficult the situation was for him, I decided to try Tonglen. The remarkable thing is that the very next day his hands returned to normal. Two days later he started working again.

Since that time I have used it many times and I share it in my workshops and meditation courses, with amazing results.

The practice can be found in various formats but one simple and very effective format is this one, used by my teachers and myself:

Find a quiet and comfortable place. Observe your breathing for a few minutes. Put your hands in the position of *namasté* (hands at heart level, palms together) and put your attention and awareness on your heart, on the point between the two halves of your ribcage.

From that place, connect with your essence, your inner source or with the heart field. State your intention to yourself and ask that this practice be of benefit to all beings without exception. Think about the person in question; a good idea is to say that person's name three times in your mind. Imagine the person in his or her current state and, as you inhale, feel that a dark cloud full of suffering and distress enters your heart. Once it is inside, feel that it is changing, as if it were burning away, and with the exhalation, return to the person a pure, white cloud that represents life and love. Imagine how the face of the person changes when he or she receives this white cloud, becoming happier and more serene. Every time you repeat the procedure, the dark clouds become lighter, moving through different shades of gray, until they become white or transparent.

If you wish, you can lower your hands to your thighs and as you inhale draw your fingers toward your palms in a closed fist, to symbolize that you are receiving the suffering of the other person. As you exhale, open them to release the blessings.

To finish, visualize that person feeling completely happy. Once again, put your hands at heart level and, from your heart, ask that the benefits of this practice reach all beings without exception.

This is a spectacular method for helping release other people's suffering and our own suffering. It enables us to apply compassion and it removes us from one of the main sources of suffering: believing that we are the center of the universe and thinking that we live in isolation and with no connection to others. This is an excellent technique for helping us escape from that "individual" mind that focuses only on itself.

So, dear friend and reader, if you have any type of discomfort, whether physical, mental or emotional, do this exercise for someone who is in equally bad or even worse shape than you. By doing so you will begin to heal. You will also observe big, wonderful blessings in your life.

(In silence, allow yourself to simply feel)

Story:

—What should my penance be, given the enormity of my offenses? —asked the disciple.

—To understand the ignorance that caused them —said the Master. Then he added:

—This way you will understand and forgive both others and yourself and you will stop asking for that vengeance you are referring to when you speak of punishment or penance.

Anthony de Mello

Chapter 11:
Getting someone out of hell

"You will teach them to fly, but they won't be flying your journey.
You will teach them to dream,
but they won't be dreaming your dream.
You will teach them to live,
but they will not live your life.
However...
in each flight, in each life, in each dream,
the imprint of the path you laid down will last".

Mother Teresa of Calcutta

Mr. Díaz was much more to me than a great teacher. I could even say that in a way he was like that father who protects you and knows how to guide you in the face of adversities. I met him by chance, or "by accident". At a social event, I somehow ended up next to a man with some very interesting proposals about improving ourselves and overcoming obstacles, about the limiting beliefs we often have and the tools we need to wake up and contribute something of value to the world.

He was born in Miami to a Canary Island-born father and a U.S.-born mother. Both of his parents worked in the business world, which gave him the opportunity to travel widely. From an early age, he often experienced panic attacks and recurring bouts of depression. He had the feeling that he did not fit in very well in this world. As time passed he began using tranquilizers and different social drugs, and he became addicted. Even so, he kept looking for meaning in his life and was always trying to move forward.

Then, at the age of 33, Mr. Díaz went through a period of absolute desperation that led him to contemplate suicide. He was determined to put an end to the life that seemed to have no meaning. So he filled the bathtub with hot water and picked up some sharp razor blades. When he was just about to slit his wrists, he somehow slipped and fell and ended up hitting his head very hard. He was lying on the floor for a few minutes when the following idea rushed into his heart: "Since I am not afraid of dying, why not devote my life to the search for answers, to mental and spiritual growth? Why waste this life if I can dedicate it to finding truth and to helping others".

That day was a turning point in the life of Mr. Díaz, who, from that time forward, sought out different teachers of Reiki, Tibetan Buddhist monks, shamans and other great meditators. This is how he became one of the most impressive Western masters I have ever met.

In this chapter I would like to share with you, dear reader, the fascinating story that allowed Mr. Díaz to become a teacher on the spiritual path that he was following.

All people who live this philosophy or path, which has been given various names and is the subject of the courses and workshops I give (in this book we will simply call it the Tibetan energy system), must pass a final test before becoming masters. To understand what this test consists of, it is sufficient to simply hear its name: "getting someone out of hell".

Mr. Díaz knew that sooner or later he would have to do this test. But he didn't know when, where or how.

It happened in 1994. Mr. Díaz was driving through one of the most problematic neighborhoods of a nearby island, when his car's engine decided that that perfectly normal day was the perfect time to stop suddenly, with no warning whatsoever, at that particular place. And why shouldn't it?

So he got out of the car and walked through the streets in search of the closest gas station. He was calm, aware, present. At about 9:30 p.m. a man who seemed to appear out of nowhere shoved him against the wall and put a syringe full of blood at his neck:

—Give me everything you've got or I'll inject you with this blood!

—What a beautiful, loving thing to do! —responded Mr. Díaz smiling at him affectionately.

—Don't you get it? I've got AIDS! —Give me all your money or I'll inject you with this! —shouted the assailant, completely disconcerted.

—I get it, but it seems to me to be a beautiful act of love that you would want to share your blood with me —Mr. Díaz repeated.

—Didn't you hear me? This blood is infected! —shouted the drug addict, in a tone revealing a combination of impatience and amazement.

—You think it's infected, but I don't. So, for me, your blood is perfect.

The attacker was now getting angry.

—Hey, you stupid hippy, this is serious! —Give me all your money or I swear I'll inject you!

—Well then, since it's money you want, take this —responded Mr. Díaz patiently while taking out his wallet and offering it kindly to his attacker.— There's about 120 Euros in there. The only thing I ask for in exchange is that you go out for dinner with me. My treat.

—But who the hell are you? The police or something? —asked the other, in total confusion.

—No, I would just like to talk with you for awhile. The money is yours. Just let me keep the ID card and the picture of my nephew. The rest you can have.

The attacker had no choice but to accept this unusual invitation from this atypical victim. With a mixture of curiosity and fear (as he would confess later), he agreed to go to a café with the man who, from that day onwards, would be considered a "master".

There they were, the attacker, who at this point didn't know what to do with the wallet, looking at Mr. Díaz as he calmly ate his sandwich, with a smile of satisfaction on his lips. They started talking. Mr. Díaz asked him to tell him a little about his life, his childhood, and how he had ended up on the streets.

From a very early age, the man had received severe beatings from his parents (he was an alcoholic, she was addicted to tranquilizers) and he was constantly told that he was useless and should never have been born.

As a teenager, he sought refuge in drugs, which made life bearable for a short while, turning his real life into a vague memory of a nightmare.

However, when the effects of the substances faded, the reality of his situation became more real and more horrible, tormenting his soul and ravaging his body. The same drugs that took him away from abuse and neglect put him in an increasingly difficult social situation, forcing him to steal, threaten, extort and commit robbery in order to obtain another dose of fictitious amnesia. His life became a constant fight for survival in which the only way to get out was to get high. The people around him were always what we tend to call "problematic" people: he was involved with many drug addicts, most of them prostitutes. At some point he was infected with HIV. Since then he lived in anger, thinking he would not hesitate an instant if he had to inject his blood into another person, something that hadn't yet occurred since —until that crazy night— all his victims had handed over the money and run away.

Mr. Díaz listened to the story attentively. When the man finished talking, Mr. Díaz asked if that way of life helped him overcome his rage, hate and unhappiness. Paco (this is the name we will give him) answered that it was the only way he knew: he knew of no other way to release all the suffering that burdened him.

Mr. Díaz told him something important: the very fact of having lived through so much suffering could make him a great teacher, someone who could help other young people going through or about to go through a similar hell. He explained to him that instead of generating so much anger, he could bring more peace and awareness to the world. To do so, he would have to realize that the real battle is inside; that is, instead of going out to fight, he would have to focus on changing himself through "self-compassion" which is something totally unrelated to feeling pity for oneself and taking the position of victim of the world and of our particular circumstances.

At that point in the evening, Paco started crying. How could he change if he was tormented, his soul was in pain, he could get no rest unless he took some sort of substance to make him sleep?

Mr. Díaz put his hand on the back of Paco's neck, comforting him for a few minutes and then he said:

—Friend, I have been through the same "hell" as you and it made me understand where "heaven" is. Come with me. You are going to discover the enormous potential that you have inside; you are going to find out who you really are.

Paco stared at him in awe, taking in Mr. Díaz' loving and compassionate gaze. So he accepted.

Now I can say that of that suffering, tormented man, there is absolutely nothing left. The transformation was spectacular. He began meditating and he learned about the Tibetan energy system that I teach in my workshops. He started working as a veterinarian's assistant and then he was trained as a nursing assistant specialized in geriatrics. Subsequent tests revealed that his blood and body had rid itself of the disharmony known as AIDS. With his experience, Paco has been of great assistance to many people who are going through, just like he was years ago, a desperate situation that seems to have no way out.

Many years passed after all this happened, and one day while I was at Mr. Díaz's house, a man arrived and came up to me. He was about fifty, had tattoos all over his hands and he couldn't stop smiling.

—You must be Manchado —he said.

—And you must be the famous Paco —I answered.

—That's right —he said laughing—. I see that Mr. Díaz has told you about me.

I realized that I had before me a wonderful and unexpected opportunity: to hear the story told from the other side, something I enjoyed immensely. I will share something funny to conclude this chapter: Paco admitted to me that when he saw Mr. Díaz and heard what he said during the attack, he actually feared for his life because he thought he had chosen a psychopath as a victim. But he decided to go have dinner with that "fearless crazy man" anyway and that dinner ended up changing his life.

There are many lessons to be learned from this story. But I would highlight this one: the greatness of getting someone out of hell simply by listening without prejudices, providing tools, applying compassion instead of judging, condemning, and setting the person aside.

(In silence, allow yourself to simply feel)

Story:

—Where should I look for illumination?

—Here.

—And when will it happen?

—It's happening right now.

—Then why can't I feel it? —Because you're not looking.

—And what should I be looking for?

—Nothing. Just look.

—But look at what?

—At whatever it is that your eyes have before them.

—Must I look at it in some special way? —No, it is enough just to look normally. —But don't I always look normally?

—No.

—And why not, damn it?

—Because to look you have to be here, and you are almost always somewhere else.

Anthony de Mello

Chapter 12:
My "strange" walks with Mr. Díaz

"The birth of man is the birth of his sorrow. The longer he lives, the more stupid he becomes, because his anxiety to avoid unavoidable death becomes more and more acute. What bitterness! He lives for what is always out of reach! His thirst for survival in the future makes him incapable of living in the present".

Chuang Tzu

As a form of instruction, Mr. Díaz, my teacher, would often take me out for walks. Together we went to many different places, and they were always interesting. On one occasion he took me to a café in Villa de Teguise, on the island of Lanzarote, where some black and white photos were on display. They were very old, probably about a hundred years old. The people in the pictures were dressed in the outfits typical of the period: some were smiling, others had serious expressions.

Mr. Díaz told me:

—Look at the pictures. Look at all of them closely and feel what they transmit to you.

And so I did. Some expressed joy, others sadness. Mr. Díaz smiled at me and continued:

Dear Manchado, here you can see images of people who lived in a state of worry, always concerned about their problems, their yearnings... A hundred years have passed and the question is: where have these worries, fears, yearnings and troubles gone? They have been taken away by impermanence, dear friend! Be aware of this: everything changes constantly, so do not waste time believing the ego and its thought system (emotional conflicts, personal conflicts, mental conflicts, relationship conflicts. Move beyond all that, and always choose to live in peace (because that is what you are: peace, love, acceptance...), with the understanding that everything is in constant flux. Make sure that every day your acceptance, your forgiveness, your non-judgment grow... Simply feel, observe everything consciously and always choose to continue discovering yourself and reconnecting more deeply with life and with your inner self. As many of my teachers say, "when death comes for you, make sure it finds you full of life".

In this case, Mr. Díaz was making literal reference to one of the basic precepts of Buddhist philosophy regarding precious human existence, so difficult to acquire yet so easy to lose, which is that we must use life to the best of our ability, developing our potential as much as we possibly can, in order to awaken our Buddha nature (which is the awakening of consciousness) and return our minds to love.

On another occasion, I spent several nights meditating with him in a cemetery. Aside from how strange or uncomfortable such an experience may seem, when looking at it with ordinary eyes, the purpose of it was to understand how short and limited our existence is. The idea is to not "postpone" your life or your happiness, but rather follow your true function or path in this life. We meditated on impermanence, on how grateful we felt to have good health and our precious human existence. We also looked neutrally at death, understanding it as a natural process that we must accept, because it is senseless to resist it. At the same time, we were breaking our taboos, beliefs or programs of fear regarding cemeteries, superstitions...

With this powerful experience, Mr. Díaz was also teaching me another basic Buddhist tenet, impermanence and death. Everything changes, nothing stays the same. Our life is as fragile as a bubble and we can never be sure when death will come... We must not waste time feeling attached to what we will certainly lose, since how long our life will last is unknown. Many masters use this practice as a means to reach this understanding. One of my Tibetan teachers, Kalu T., lived in a cemetery for about two years, in an effort to fully absorb the concept of death and impermanence.

Mr. Díaz also took me to hospitals, to spend time with people who were dealing with physical challenges. Before we went into the rooms, he always said:

—Do not look at them as sick people, because if you do you too will get sick, and that will be no help at all. Accept their condition, do not resist it. People who are in that state called *illness* have an absence of love towards themselves and towards the world; for this reason life gives them a disharmony or health challenge so that they can reconnect with the love that lies within them, but is covered by and hidden behind fear, guilt, anger, resentment and other toxic emotions of devaluation. You cannot help them if you see them as sick people. Observe them with total acceptance, beyond your idea or ideas about the symptoms they are displaying.

I entered the hospital with that intention. Truly, in those corridors, in those first few experiences, it was very hard for me to see them without illness. And then all of a sudden one day I could do it... It was wonderful to be able to talk with them without feeling distress or rejection of the illness! I could perceive the deep love that life itself and the Universe felt for these beings, who had been given these experiences for the sole reason of reconnecting them with life, with love and with themselves. I saw them with absolute compassion. It was not pity, but rather compassion, which in Tibetan is understood as "helping others to stop suffering". I talked with them without fear and without judging their condition. I asked them:

—What would you most like?

They responded with statements such as: "To turn back the clock and start over again" or "not to have burned my health by feeling so angry with the world" and "not to have spent my life working in something I hate..."

Others, some with reduced mobility and confined to a wheelchair, said they would give their life and all of their belongings to be able to walk for a few hours by the sea or in the countryside.

Illness and death cease to affect us when we look at them with acceptance and not with resignation or resistance. Understanding that illness, according to my teachers and to my own experiences, is a gift given by life to help you reconnect with it, to clear your anger, your resentment, your feeling of powerlessness, your resistance to love, your hate, your judgments, your feelings of guilt.

Understanding that its function is simply to return your life to love, acceptance, understanding, compassion, freedom, sharing...

If we understand all this, many fears will disappear, such as distress in the face of illness or death. As the great psychologist Carl G. Jung said, "illness is nature's attempt to heal man".

I would like to discuss another concept that, according to all my Tibetan teachers, we are experiencing if we see life from a perspective that is overly-identified with forms, with the ego and its thought system: the suffering of existence. The essence of our existence is suffering. We suffer when we are born, when we grow old, when we fall ill and when we die. People who don't have something tend to suffer to attain it; those who have little suffer because they want more; those who have enough suffer to keep what they have...And in the end we all lose whatever it is that we have. This is the reason we must try to transcend this existence.

And finally I would like to share the wisdom of this Buddhist text about impermanence, Anitya:

> "All that is born must die,
> all that is accumulated must be dispersed,
> all that is built must collapse
> and all that has been high must fall"

(In silence, allow yourself to simply feel)

Story:

A six-year-old girl was working hard on a picture. The teacher went up to her and asked:

—What are you drawing?

—I am drawing a picture of God —said the little girl. —But nobody knows what God looks like!

—They will in a minute! —responded the little girl.

Ken Robinson, in his book *"The Element"*

Chapter 13: The internal GPS

"All human beings are born with an innate
wisdom for recognizing negative emotions".

Tulku Lobsang Rinpoche

Mr. Díaz always reminded his 5-year-old nephew, Victor, how important it is to pay attention to how we feel: he worked hard to teach him to listen to and identify his emotions and, especially, to allow himself to be guided by his feelings.

One day, a teacher who was on duty during recess heard an interesting conversation between Victor and another boy who was two years older. In this conversation, the older boy had the idea of breaking a window so that they could sneak into a room at the back of the school, where certain toys were stored. After listening to this boy's plan, Victor closed his eyes for a moment. Then he opened them and answered:

—No, thanks. My internal GPS tells me that it isn't right.

The other boy tried to convince him. What do you mean your internal GPS? That's ridiculous! They had to do it right then, when nobody was looking! But Victor, to the teacher's amazement, thought again for a few seconds and said:

—No way! I'm not doing it!

—You're such a sissy! Come on, don't be a 'fraidy cat. —he insisted, this time with a more threatening tone of voice.

—Now my internal GPS is telling me 'not a chance in this world'!
—Victor rushed to say. —And get away from me, you are bad company!

The teacher was very impressed by how such a young child had handled the situation, and she wanted to know more about the internal GPS.

She called the boy's family, and they quickly put her in touch with his uncle, Mr. Díaz. He explained to her how important it is to know how to listen to and manage one's emotions, and how all this knowledge can be transmitted to children using the image of an internal GPS.

The teacher began teaching her class this method of self-guidance based on how we feel. After working like this for some time, she noticed many positive changes and, even more importantly, she found that many children with attention deficit and hyperactivity began to improve and make progress thanks to this method. It is wonderful to see how a child can serve as an example for other people around him, and how this kind of teaching can benefit all beings without exception.

What do the masters say?

Within us we have a gift that the Universe gave us to keep us connected with life: our innermost feeling. This innermost feeling serves as an indicator (sort of an internal GPS) that shows us where we are and how disconnected we are from our path, which is simply to live in peace and be connected with love.

When we talk about our innermost feeling, we can distinguish two types: one that is connected to peace (Love) and one that indicates that we are in conflict (fear).

When we notice sensations of contraction, we are in the midst of a conflictive feeling; however, when we are connected to a feeling of peace, what we notice is expansion... and we know we are on the right path!

Our innermost feeling is our most reliable informant. It lets us know what type of perception we are using at any given moment: this perception can be either erroneous (one based on judgment, rejection, etc.) or it can be compassionate (innocent perception, that of appreciation).

When we are very mental, we disconnect ourselves from our innermost feeling and we may even go so far as to cast judgment on it. In so doing, we disconnect from the main purpose of being alive: experiencing the world through our innermost feeling.

The mantra of these great teachers is: "right now I let myself feel".

What do the masters do?

They totally accept their innermost feeling, allowing it to simply be.

They always connect with the innermost feeling without interpreting it mentally. They guide their actions with this natural internal GPS.

They accept each emotion as a great messenger or indicator of where they are and what type of perception of the world they are using.

They let go of the mind so as to enter the field of the heart and connect with their inner feeling.

They allow life to express itself through their innermost feeling.

What do the masters not do?

They do not analyze or question their innermost feeling. They do not judge it.

They are not mental nor do they allow themselves to be influenced by the conflict-oriented mindset. They do not try to control their innermost feeling.

They do not put up resistance or deny their emotions.

They do not repress or cancel out their innermost feeling with prescription drugs or illegal substances.

Practice:

In a quiet place, observe what kind of innermost feeling is moving within you. Accept it and understand that it is talking to you about those aspects of life in which you are connected to or disconnected from love.

If you detect an intense emotion, ask yourself from the heart: "At this time, what does life want to transmit to me through this feeling?"

And wait, observing how you feel in silence, for the answer to rise up spontaneously from your innermost feeling.

Poem:

Your children are
not your children.
They are the sons

and daughters of Life's
longing for itself.
They come through
you but not from you,

And though they are
with you, they belong not to you
You may give them your

love but not your thoughts.
For they have their own thoughts.
You may house their bodies
but not their souls.
For their souls dwell in
the house of tomorrow,

which you cannot visit,
not even in your dreams.
You may strive to be like them,

but seek not to make them like you.
For life goes not backward
nor tarries with yesterday.
You are the bows from which your children as living arrows are sent forth.
Let your bending in the archer's hand be for gladness.

Khalil Gibran

Chapter 14:
Helping children stay connected

"Everybody is a genius. But if you judge a fish by its ability to climb a tree, it will live its whole life believing that it is stupid".

Unknown, although often attributed to Albert Einstein

*"The way we were treated as children is the way
we will treat ourselves for the rest of our lives".*

Alice Miller

*"If there is anything we wish to change in the child, we should first examine it and
see whether it is not something that could be better changed in ourselves".*

Carl G. Jung

Albert was a very sensitive and intuitive child. He lived in a house in the country, in an exceptional spot, nestled among mountains and trees, with a little stream gurgling nearby.

At the age of five, he already enjoyed nature a great deal and considered it a gift. He went outside whenever his parents allowed him to. Even at such a young age, he was thrilled to breathe the fresh air of the countryside, which he loved. His enjoyment of nature was very deep and whenever he had the chance he spent time outdoors, playing with butterflies and trees, listening to the chirping of birds, the murmur of running water...

Albert clearly had a special sensitivity. He remembers that sometimes, when he was little, the trees spoke to him, and he was always enthralled by it. One day he was so enthusiastic about what the trees had told him that he wanted to share it with his parents. But it seems that they did not take it with the same joy and enthusiasm as little Albert. At the beginning they simply attributed it to their child's vivid imagination. But when he insisted, they reacted more harshly: they warned him not to be silly and say such stupid things again, or people would think he was crazy.

He couldn't understand all those mean and scornful words: stupid, crazy, silly... The message transmitted by the trees was fabulous! And he wanted his parents to know about it, but this time they responded with violence. Fearing the neighbors would think that their son was a weirdo, someone who talked to himself, they beat him severely, and this was followed by more beatings whenever he talked about the message of the trees. This continued until the child ended up "interpreting" the situation to mean that he had to stop. He could not keep listening to nature. Why not? He didn't really understand. But he could not take any more of these harsh reactions from his parents... whose words were as damaging as the blows.

His confusion gave way to guilt, fear and even to feelings of anger at himself for not fitting into the mold, for not being the child his parents wanted him to be. He spent almost fifty years rejecting the gift he had been given. He lived a painful life of disconnection, lies, falseness. He could only pretend to be someone he was not, to play a role that pleased his family, his friends, his surroundings, society...

But everything has a limit. Tired of suffering in his constant search for approval, he decided to simply give up. He tore down all the barriers that had been placed around him since he was small, he reconnected with nature and his essential innocence. He accepted his gift, that great sensitivity that only very exceptional people can understand, or at least respect. And he went to live among the trees, which is what his inner nature had been telling him to do all the while.

And I know that he is now very happy. The time that has passed is not important. He feels that he is once again a child.

What do the masters say?

Children come into this world fully connected to life and to the source. They bring with them incredible joy and innate wisdom. They show great enthusiasm and spontaneity, which they are eager to share, and they live almost in a state of ecstasy. They arrive knowing how to breathe and with correct posture. Even when they get hurt, they put their hands over the painful area as if they were practicing Reiki or some other energy technique.

The writer Gerald Jampolsky tells a real story about a three-year-old girl who asks to be left alone for a moment with her newborn baby brother. Their parents, somewhat surprised by this request, agree to the plan, but they stay close enough to be able to hear, in amazement, what the girl says:

—Baby, tell me about God, I am starting to forget...

Children are here to live the present intensely: to play, enjoy, explore... Their greatest treasure is their innocence.

The teacher Mr. Díaz says: "children are completely sure that they are here to have a good time, it is us adults who get them off track".

Since they are innocent (they do not have installed beliefs), children are able to see, hear, feel and perceive what adults cannot.

What do the masters do?

They show patience, understanding and connection with their children at all times.

They teach their children through love, trust and respect.

They let their children flow naturally and they teach them to feel their emotions without judging them.

They allow them to develop their natural talents, their creative and artistic abilities.

They pay attention and are fully present, responding to them with patience and serenity.

They encourage them to live freely, without fear, without coercion and without conditions.

They reinforce their self-esteem and their inner power, promoting in them the idea that everything in life is possible if you set your mind to it.

They encourage them to understand that we are all connected and we are one with everything.

They nourish their spirits with attention and approval. Every day they see their children with new eyes, unfettered by the past.

What do the masters not do?

They never disconnect their children from the wisdom, innocence and sensitivity within them.

They do not force them to adhere to what is supposedly "normal," by not accepting their sensitivity or their gifts.

They do not raise them in competition, anger, fear, devaluation.

They do not teach them separation or "indiviDUALism". They do not say negative things to them.

They do not devalue them.

They do not scold them for following how they feel.

They do not get angry with them for imagining or playing.

They do not talk to them as if they were stupid, but rather as what they are: potential wise people.

They do not hit them or insult them.

In some of my workshops on happiness, I have put out the following question to get a feeling for the state of mind of the participants:

—OK, guys, how many of you believe yourselves to be wonderful people who deserve the very best?

Usually, nobody answers, so I try again, with a big smile on my face:
—Come on, don't be shy!

I repeat the question: among all of you in this room, who believes that you are a wonderful person who deserves the very best?

At this point, someone always starts to raise a hand but when they feel observed by the others, they immediately transform the action into a not-very-subtle contortion, an awkward movement intended to make people think they are stretching, scratching their head or smoothing their hair.

At this point I feign surprise and I tell them:

—Hey, people! What's happened to you? Just yesterday I asked the same question at a primary school and all the children stood up shouting and jumping up and down!

Some of my teachers say that an adult is a child who has forgotten how to smile. They also say that an adult is an "adulterated" child. Others are harsher, and consider adults to be children that have been "ruined". Some of them even say that adults are like broken toys. Dear reader/child, I have good news for you! What is forgotten can be remembered, what is ruined can be fixed and what is broken can be repaired. Get back that smile, get back that inner child who is waiting to be rescued and then, once you are a child again, you will enter the "kingdom of heaven" (true happiness without conditions).

Before this chapter ends, so that we can see just how connected children are, I am going to quickly share the case of a woman who came to see me because she was worried about her son, who apparently talked to himself...

When the mother and children came into the office, I found a child aged around 5, with a sweet face and big, shining, peaceful eyes. I asked the mother what was happening and she anxiously responded that the child spent a lot of time talking to an invisible friend.

I looked at the child and asked him:

—Well, who is your invisible friend?

—God —responded the little boy, to the great surprise of his mother, who had never bothered to ask him this question.

I smiled and asked:

—And what does God say to you?

—That everything is all right and not to worry.

When I asked him what God is like he told me that He has no shape. Finally, when I wanted to know where God was at the moment, the child, quite naturally, said:

—Here! Mixed up with everything!

Practice:

Seated in a meditation position, breathe in deeply at least three times, while saying the following:

—I let go of everything false that disconnects me from life. Those projections are not me, they are not real.

Focus your attention on your heart, on the spot between the two halves of your ribcage, for several minutes or longer. Then make the following affirmations:

As you inhale: *"I reconnect with the innocence and freshness that is within me"*. As you exhale: *"I see everything with the joy and enthusiasm of a child"*.

Finally, say thank you for this new day. And express your hope that this meditation will benefit all beings without exception.

A few words on love:

They made us believe that real love, the one that's strong, only happens once, most likely before your thirties. They never told us that love is not something that you can put in motion or that has a time schedule.

They made us believe that each one of us is half an orange, and that life only makes sense when you find the other half. They did not tell us that we were born whole, and that no one else in our lives deserves to carry on their back the responsibility of completing what is missing in us: we grow through life by ourselves. If we have good company, it's just more pleasant.

They made us believe in a kind of "two in one" formula: two people sharing the same line of thinking, the same ideas, and that it is what works. It's never been said that that has another name: invalidation, that only two individuals with their own personality can have a healthy relationship. They made us believe that marriage is a necessary institution and that fantasies at the wrong time should be repressed.

They made us believe that the thin and beautiful are the ones who are most loved, that the ones who have little sex are boring, and the ones who have a lot of it are not trustworthy, and that there will always be an old shoe for a crooked foot; what they forgot to tell us is that there are more crooked minds than crooked feet.

They made us believe that there's only one way, one formula, to be happy, the same way for everybody, and those that escape from it are destined to be delinquents. We have never been told that those formulas go wrong, they get people frustrated, they are alienating, and that we can try other alternatives. Oh! And they did not tell us that no one will tell us these things. Each and every one of us will have to learn by ourselves.

And, it is only when we love ourselves that can we fall in love with somebody else.

Author unknown

Chapter 15:
Love: unconscious relationships

"You must love in such a way that the person you love feels free".

Thich Nhat Hanh

*"Remember that the best relationship is one in which
your love for each other exceeds your need for each other".*

Dalai Lama

"Your inner peace is driving me crazy".

My ex-girlfriend

I met Juan in 1998 and he soon became a close friend. He was an up-and-coming salesman at a well-known Spanish company and he was on holiday with some friends, trying to disconnect a bit from the busy, stressful lives they lived in the city. He had already been thinking for some time about the possibility of a change of scene and when he discovered the small island called La Graciosa, he felt one hundred percent sure about it. So, he returned to his city, turned in a letter of resignation and, after saying goodbye to his friends and family, grabbed his bags and settled into a remote corner of the island.

There he started to live the life he had always dreamed of, devoting body and soul to the activities he truly loved: sports, meditation and yoga, surfing... He noticed that day by day he was becoming more and more connected with his inner self. For the first time in years he was truly happy: he knew he was in the right place, enjoying this wonderful communion with his surroundings. He felt really alive, and perhaps for the first time since he was born, he was aware of his breathing and of the beating of his heart. And all of these sensations were growing. He felt so inspired that he even began to write a book about meditation and its connection with nature.

One afternoon, while he was on the beach with his surfboard, he saw two young women walk by. One of them immediately grabbed his attention. She was lovely, a "goddess" thought Juan at the time. Her face, her body, the rhythm as she walked, the long hair cascading down her back, the way she tossed the lock of hair away from her lips... Everything about her was perfect! When he saw that they were heading toward him and she asked him for a light, he felt he could barely breathe. They lit a cigarette and chatted for a few minutes, a brief conversation that helped Juan put his feet back on the ground: hiding behind that appearance of *femme fatale* was a little girl, with many stories inside her that needed to be worked out. It would be best to let her go... Yes, he thought, they were on completely different wavelengths. However, there was another part of him that couldn't stop thinking about those big eyes of hers...

The next day, the two young women came back, and the one he liked made it very clear that she had a certain interest in my friend. That very night they began a passionate romance that would lead Juan, as he put it, to take giant steps away from his dream.

Soon they decided to live together in a larger apartment, but that resulted in them often being short of money. The solution was to move to a bigger island where Juan could find work more easily. There was no longer time for surfing or for yoga, and his book was forgotten at the back of a drawer.

His girlfriend had an extravagant lifestyle that he, out of love, tried to follow for some time: fancy clothes, nightlife, dinner parties... However, it was never enough for him. Inside he began to feel an indescribable anguish. He tried to hide his distress behind the love he felt for her: a love that, supposedly, should have been enough to justify such a sacrifice.

When his girlfriend became pregnant, Juan had to work extra hours. He was tired. Something inside him kept reminding him of his dream, telling him repeatedly that this was not the life for him. The feeling became stronger and it came more often. To make the little voice go away, and also to be able to handle his long work days, Juan began taking drugs.

The birth of his daughter was a joyful event for him, but also a new responsibility; a responsibility that, it turned out, was also too much for the mother, who showed little interest in the baby. This situation added a huge additional weight to Juan's already exhausted shoulders. How long ago were those days of surfing on the beaches of La Graciosa! Although in a certain way the laughter and the time he spent with his daughter helped him forget the failing relationship, which was going from bad to worse.

Despite the huge efforts that Juan was making, his girlfriend was aggressive and distant. She was often out and during the rare times that she was at home, she treated him like he was a nuisance. The relationship became colder and colder, and there was no contact between the two of them. Juan tried visiting various psychologists and he even tried various medications. Shortly after that, he found out his girlfriend was sleeping around. One day, he simply couldn't take it anymore: in a state of severe depression, unable to get out of bed, he had to be taken to the emergency room.

When he was released, he decided to spend a week on La Graciosa with his surfboard as his only company. There he once again had that great feeling of expansion that he had discovered years before and he realized that a huge smile was beginning to grow inside him. He heard a phrase deep inside him, waking him up right away: "If it is distress that you feel, what you are receiving is not love. Open your eyes!"

Suddenly, he connected with what he really was and realized that what he had been living was a "non-life". So he decided to return to Gran Canaria for a short time. There, he embraced his girlfriend and thanked her for all that he had learned during their years together, he said goodbye to his daughter and he started travelling the world with his surfboard in his arms: Sri Lanka, Bali, Australia, the Philippines, Mexico...

Of course, he always stayed close to the love of his life, his daughter Eliana. As soon as the little girl was old enough to understand, Juan told her the whole story. The last time I saw them together, Eliana, who is now ten, told me proudly that her father was her favorite superhero.

What do the masters say?

The reason for suffering in relationships is that we are looking outside for what we have not found inside. We are looking outside for what we are denying to ourselves. If we feel separate and we do not love ourselves, we end up looking all over the place, like beggars, for love outside of us... And in exchange we sacrifice our freedom. Jesus, as a teacher, said this: "Love your neighbor as you love yourself". This phrase puts it nicely: love yourself first and then, to the same degree, love someone else...Not the other way around! In addition, a deep-seated fear of solitude pushes us to find someone who will always stay by our side. As a result, we confuse love with need and we generate attachment and dependence.

When attachment occurs, we exaggerate the characteristics of persons or objects, distorting our perception to the point that we give them qualities they do not possess; we become dependent on the idea we have created in our minds, and we believe that without that person we cannot be happy. In this madness that makes us dependent, we are willing to give up our true nature, our values and even our inner path, all in order to please someone else, to try to ensure that the person never leaves us, since we think that he or she is the source of all our happiness. This is where expressions such as: "I'll die if you leave me" or "my life has no meaning without you" come from. In most cases, this type of person ends up being rejected by his or her beloved, because the beloved cannot take the pressure of being the other person's sole source of happiness.

With this idea of conditioned love experienced through the filters of a conflict-oriented mindset, the relationship becomes a power struggle that simply reflects our own fears and state of mind.

Contrary to popular belief, relationships do not bring happiness: they are actually a complement that enhances the happiness already existing, or a big mirror showing our reflection.

To have a satisfying relationship, the key is non-attachment. This does not mean that our relationship is cold or distant, but rather that our mindset is calm, happy, present, unfettered by worries or by thoughts that the person belongs to us, and also that we see everything with clarity, without dependence, with understanding and even without fear. The Spanish writer and yoga teacher Ramiro Calle has come up with an excellent definition of non-attachment:

Non-attachment is not the denial of desire, but rather not being tied to it; it means being able to be happy even if you do not get what you want. Non-attachment leads to acceptance: it is not resignation but rather patience in action, it is understanding that we cannot change everything but that we can always change ourselves. Attachment is need, and need always distances you from what you want.

The ultimate goal of a relationship is for two people to evolve or grow together, to share happiness and to help each other remember their true nature, which is Love. The presence of pain and suffering is a clear indicator that we are not in a loving relationship but rather in some distorted or conditioned idea of a relationship, a reflection of our emotional poverty and fear.

What do the masters do?

Their relationships are unconditional.

They understand that in the relative world in which we live relationships are marvelous mirrors in which we can discover ourselves.

They understand that a relationship serves to strengthen our true nature, which is Love.

They are conscious that to achieve complete harmony it is important to be with someone we connect with at the spiritual, mental and physical levels.

They keep their freedom in a non-conditioned relationship, because that is the nature of love.

They grow together (forming a couple, having children...).

They share happiness.

They do not create illusions, but they are enthusiastic about their relationships.

What do the masters not do?

They do not have a relationship that works against their nature or their path. They do not sacrifice their path or their values for a relationship.

They do not have a conditioned relationship.

They do not sacrifice their freedom (Love is freedom).

They do not resign themselves to a relationship that has no understanding or harmony, simply out of fear (fear of what people will think, or fear of being alone...).

They do not have a relationship characterized by attachment or dependency.

They do not give up their function in life for a relationship. They do not devalue themselves or others in the relationship. They are not entirely wrapped up in the other person.

They do not stop being themselves in an attempt to be the other person's ideal.

They do not try to force the other person to be or to act as they would like them to.

Practice:

Sit in a comfortable, quiet place:

As you inhale, feel or visualize how a sort of shining white or golden cloud comes inside you through your nose and fills you up with life and freedom. As you exhale, feel a black cloud leaving you, taking with it all your attachment, dependence or addiction toward a person, object, situation, place, etc.

Repeat this breathing cycle 7 times. With each exhale, put all of your attention on the cloud and really feel that it is leaving your body.

Notice that it becomes clearer each time, until it turns white or transparent.

Sit in meditation for a few minutes, observing how you feel.

Finally, hope that the benefits of this meditation will reach all beings without exception.

Story:

A man found an eagle's egg and put it in the nest of a barnyard hen. The eaglet hatched with the brood of chicks and grew up with them. All his life the eagle did what the barnyard chicks did, thinking he was a barnyard chicken. He scratched the earth for worms and insects. He clucked and cackled. And he would thrash his wings and fly a few feet into the air.

Years passed and the eagle grew very old. One day he saw a magnificent bird above him in the cloudless sky. It glided in graceful majesty among the powerful wind currents, with scarcely a beat on his strong golden wings.

The old eagle looked up in awe. "Who's that?" he asked. "That's the eagle, the king of the birds," said his neighbor. "He belongs to the sky. We belong to the earth - we're chickens." So the eagle lived and died a chicken, for that's what he thought he was.

Anthony de Mello

Chapter 16:
The mouse and learned fears

"Love is what we are born with. Fear is what we learn. The spiritual journey is the unlearning of fear and prejudices and the acceptance of love back in our hearts. Love is the essential reality and our purpose on earth. To be consciously aware of it, to experience love in ourselves and others, is the meaning of life. Meaning does not lie in things. Meaning lies in us".

Marianne Williamson

In this chapter, my dear friend and student Sonia Rivas tells us a story about herself:

I was very little. I would have been about three. I know because my grandmother died right around that time. I remember the day well. Also, my mother often tells the story at family gatherings. I had gone with my parents and my maternal grandparents to visit a small vineyard that my parents owned. In the middle there was a little country house. Since I was so little, while my parents and grandparents were outside, they left me playing inside. I was entertaining myself when suddenly I saw a mouse running by the wall, near the fireplace I didn't think anything of it and kept playing. After a while, I went out on the porch and joined my family. At one point, when my mother suggested we all go in the house, I informed them that there were mice inside. My mother and grandmother paid no attention:

—What would such a little girl know about mice! —they said to each other.

The funny thing was that when my mother went in the house and saw the mouse, she climbed up on a chair and started screaming. I looked at her and, since I didn't know what to do, I decided to act the same way as she did. So there we were, the two of us, up high, one on the couch and the other on a chair, waving our hands around and shrieking like madwomen. The little mouse, of course, ran away. After a little while, when things had calmed down, my mother looked at me and said:

—Why is it that when you saw the mouse the first time you thought nothing of it and the second time you wouldn't stop screaming?

My response was this:

—Ah, it's because I didn't know that mice are something to be scared of.

Story:

A young man went to talk to a great master and said to him:

—Master, I have come to see you because I feel like a nobody and I have no strength to do anything. Everyone says that I am useless, clumsy and stupid, that I am no good at anything. How can I improve? What can I do so that people will appreciate me more?

Without looking at him the master said:

—I'm very sorry but I can't help you, I must first solve my own problem. Maybe later...—and then, after a pause, he added:— If you would like to help me, I might reach a solution faster and then perhaps I could help you.

—I'm happy to help, master —stammered the young man, but he felt that once again he was not being valued and his needs were being set aside.

—Fine —agreed the master. He removed the ring he was wearing on the little finger of his left hand and he gave it to the young man. —Take the horse tied up outside and go quickly to the market. I must sell this ring because I have to pay a debt. You must try to get as much as you can for it, certainly not less than a gold coin. Go quickly and come back with that coin as fast as you can.

The young man took the ring and left.

As soon as he reached the market he started offering the ring to the merchants there. They looked at the ring with certain interest, until the young man told them what he wanted for it.

When the young man mentioned the gold coin, some of the merchants laughed, others turned away and only one old man was kind enough to take the time to explain that a gold coin was much too valuable to exchange it for a ring. Someone, trying to be nice, offered him a silver coin and a copper pot for it but the young man had instructions not to accept anything less than a gold coin, and so he rejected the offer.

After offering the ring to everybody he saw at the market —more than one hundred people— and feeling dejected because of his failure, he mounted his horse and went back.

How the young man wished that he himself had a gold coin! He could have then given it to the master to free him from his worries and then receive his help and advice.

He went into the room.

—Master —he said—, I'm sorry, what you asked for is not possible. I might be able to get two or three silver coins, but I don't think I could deceive anybody about the real value of the ring.

—What you are saying is very important, my young friend —answered the master smilingly—. We must first find out the ring's real value. Get back on the horse and go to the jeweler. Who better than the jeweler to tell us its value? Tell him that you want to sell the ring and ask him how much he would give you for it. But it doesn't matter how much he offers, you don't sell it. Come back here with my ring.

The young man galloped away.

The jeweler examined the ring under the light, he looked at it with a magnifying glass, he weighed it and finally he said:

—Young man, tell the master that if he wants to sell it immediately, I cannot give him more than 58 gold coins for his ring.

—58 gold coins! —exclaimed the youth.

—Yes —replied the jeweler. —I know that with a little time we could get about 70 coins for it, but right now, if it is an urgent sale...

The young man ran to the master's house in great excitement to tell him what had happened.

—Sit down —said the master after listening to him. —You are like this ring: a treasure, unique and valuable. And as such, only a true expert can appraise your value. Why are you going through life trying to get ordinary people to discover your true value?

And upon saying this, he put the ring back on the little finger of his left hand.

Chapter 17: Being oneself and not imitating anybody

"Lifetimes of ignorance have brought us to identify the whole of our being with ego. Its greatest triumph is to inveigle us into believing its best interests are our best interests, and even into identifying our very survival with its own. This is a savage irony, considering that ego and its grasping are at the root of all our suffering.
Yet, ego is so terribly convincing, and we have been its dupe for so long, that the thought that we might ever become egoless terrifies us. To be egoless, ego whispers to us, is to lose all the rich romance of being human, to be reduced to a colorless robot or a brain-dead vegetable".

Sogyal Rinpoche

"We are born as originals, but we die as copies".

Carl G. Jung

One day I was on the beach playing soccer with my nephew David, who would have been about six or seven at the time. I was the goalkeeper and he was shooting penalty kicks at the goal. Each time he shot, he cheered himself on, taking the name of some famous player from that period. When he was getting ready to shoot, he supplied the second-by-second commentary:

—And now Ronaldinho approaches the goal and shoots! Beckham gives the ball a tremendous kick. Zidane is going to score a goal!

He kicked the ball with all his might but I also did my best to stop it. The poor kid was getting desperate when I had the following idea:

—Hey, how about David taking a shot?

—David who? —he asked in surprise.

—Isn't your name David?

—Yes...

—Well, you, of course!

—Oh! And what team am I on?

—Where are you? In Arrecife, right? So you play on the Arrecife team-it occurred to me to tell him.

His face changed in a second.

He got the ball ready and kicked it. This time the shot was completely different. I let the ball go in the goal, doing a little theater-acting so it wouldn't be too obvious. He jumped up and down, laughing, and exclaimed: Yay! I did it! I scored!

The following shots were much more confident. So much so that I didn't have to "let them" make it to the goal... I had to work pretty hard to stop them.

Afterwards, we played a match against some other kids, who normally would have crushed him. But that day my nephew was euphoric. The other kids were all wearing t-shirts with the names of major soccer teams and they identified themselves with the players who were most popular at the time...

—I'm Beckham—said one.

—And I'm Ronaldinho— exclaimed another. —And who are you? —they asked my nephew —David! —he answered.

And David ran like never before. The others were perplexed: they noticed that something had changed. And it really had changed: it was David, the real David, who was playing. That day he won the game but even more important than that was that my nephew had connected with something immense inside him, something beyond his name: his own inner greatness.

What do the masters say?

It is vital that we connect with our inner nature and let ourselves be our own selves, not following any image, behavior pattern or automatic action, in order to not end up imitating or adopting someone else's program, such as that of a family member, a celebrity or a leader that we admire. If we do that, we are putting limitations on our freedom, since what we really need is to let go of everything that separates us from our true nature, and not to add more separation.

Also very important is not following other people's idea of success, but rather pursuing our own dreams and purpose in life.

When you connect with your inner greatness, you live a full, authentic life.

As children, we are often told to "go out in the world and become someone". This leads to disconnection and to our becoming something that has nothing to do with us.

We create a "character" based on an image we deem suitable and we seek to please others under this need to be someone special. This attitude derives from a conflict-oriented mindset that is lacking in love. We live an idea of ourselves, not what we really are inside, which is always greater than any limited idea.

By being ourselves, we are able to connect with our own greatness and with our inner teacher; this way, we can stop begging life to give us something and we can stop trying to appear a certain way, hiding behind masks that make us suffer and that disconnect us from our inner power.

The very word "liberation" tells us to be "liberated from action," suggesting that we free ourselves from actions (of trying to imitate, please, convince, influence, struggle...) and simply let go of everything false that separates us from our freedom.

As the great Padampa Sangye said:

"In a state of *natural spontaneity*, train in being free of any holding back".

What do the masters do?

They allow themselves to simply be. They are authentic.
They let go of everything false (everything not related to their own nature). They connect with their true essence.

They are themselves in every situation. They are natural and spontaneous. They live in harmony with how they feel.

What do the masters not do?

They do not imitate any guru or teacher...

They do not try to please others or be liked.

They do not seek admiration or recognition, but rather their own contentment. They do not act (artificially or sanctimoniously).

They do not seek refuge or identify with an image.

They do not make demands or impose their necessities and expectations on the present moment.

They do not create or act like a certain character or idea.

Practice:

In meditation, look into your heart. Take a few seconds to simply feel. You can make the following statements to yourself:

"Right here and now, I have decided to connect deeply with my essence and my inner self. I am deciding only to feel, to let go of interpretations, opinions, thoughts... I am letting go of everything. I choose peace and I free myself from any action, since peace is my natural state".

Just sit for a while feeling in silence, without interpreting, simply allowing yourself to feel everything as it is.

And then say:

"I am going home, I am at home".

Finally, reaffirm your hope that this practice will bring benefits to all beings without exception.

Story:

There was a teacher who one day encouraged one of his disciples to walk through a forest with him. While the teacher walked calmly, whistling softly and observing the trees and birds they saw along the way, his companion seemed tense and restless. He had no idea where they were going. Finally, tired of waiting, the disciple broke the silence and asked the teacher:

—Where are we going?

And the teacher, with a kind smile on his face, told him: —We are already there.

Chapter 18:
Impatience, the mother of insanity

"Patience does not mean enduring something and putting up with it until I can't take it any more and then exploding. Patience is the art of freeing myself of unnecessary emotional burdens in order to maintain my state of peace".

Guido Rosas

In a world in which we want everything to move quickly and in which we have a deep-rooted dislike for waiting (because our conflict-oriented programs are constantly telling us not to waste time), impatience has become one of the major causes of suffering: it produces stress, taut nerves, relationship problems, etc.

We have all heard the saying "patience is the mother of science..." Perhaps it refers to patience playing a major role in the science of being at peace with oneself, or the science of feeling truly alive and in harmony with the world. This is so true that with my own eyes I have seen people become ill as a result of impatience.

All the teachers I have met have highlighted the importance of developing patience. But what is patience? It is a state of acceptance, of non-resistance, of knowing that there is a path to travel, that a maturation process must occur before any fruit can be gathered. When we plant a tree or a flower, we do not dig it up every few days to see how it is getting along... We simply enjoy the process. Many of us know about the bamboo phenomenon: it can take up to seven years for this species to sprout, but once it has come through the soil it often grows quickly to reach a height of 30 meters.

All of my teachers suggested that I make the most of everyday life to grow, to develop different virtues, including patience. They consider life to be something like a big spiritual or psychological gym. One of the practices that some lamas recommended for working on this issue is to go to places where there tend to be long lines of people (such as the bank or the post office). Once there I was supposed to observe, both my own reactionary mind and the attitudes of others. I was instructed to wait in line and just when it was about to be my turn, to go back to the end of the line again.

So I did it and I must say that I learned a lot. I became aware of how we all go to a place with the intention of getting through as soon as possible and we even look at others with scorn, sometimes without realizing it, and if many people are waiting we tend to feel resistance and see others as an obstacle that prevents us from getting what we want: to have our turn immediately, to not waste time, to be first...

You could say we are in "I, me and my" mode: I want it to be my turn, me first, I want to go next, I have no time to waste, I don't want anybody to cut in front of me, I, me, my... Sometimes we even go so far as to speak meanly to others, since our indiviDUAL mind believes that it is more important than the rest and therefore it should be able to go first.

So, that day I went to the bank determined to put this learning into practice. Back then there were no "take a number" systems so I simply got in line and started observing myself. I noticed a certain resistance but I didn't allow myself to identify with it, I just let it flow. When it was about to be my turn, I went to the end of the line again. My mental program resisted when I let those twenty or so people go ahead of me: at first I was annoyed, even angry... so when I made it up to the front a second time, once again, I moved to the end of the line. This time, a feeling of peace came over me: I had gotten through that conflict, struggle and resistance. And each time I went to the end of the line, I felt more calm and relaxed.

As an anecdote, I will say that the third time I went to the end of that long line someone asked me if I disliked the employee at the window. I said no, I hadn't even had the pleasure of meeting her, yet!

—So what's going on? Are you shy?

—Yes, perhaps I am —I answered, smiling to myself.

We both laughed out loud and I ended up telling the person what it was that I was doing and she said with surprise:

—My goodness! You must have incredible patience and a lot of free time to be able to do such strange things!

What do the masters say?

Mainly they say that patience is the antidote to anger, which is certainly one of the mind's most harmful poisons.

Patience is an indicator that we are connected with the present moment and with love.

Patience is living in acceptance, which means assuming where we are.

Behind impatience is fear, anger, rejection, frustration, arrogance...

One phrase that they repeat often and that has to do with patience and inner peace is: "Whatever you resist, persists; whatever you complain about, stays, and whatever you love, heals".

Feeling patience is a sign that we have faith and confidence in life; the opposite is impatience.

It is a state of flow and respect for natural processes. Patience is love.

Patience is peace.

Patience is having confidence in and walking hand-in-hand with life.

What do the masters do?

They accept whatever situation they face (they assume it). They allow each situation to be as it is.

With self-observation, they affectionately monitor their state of patience.

They live in acceptance of what is.

They have respect.

They flow.

They let go of control and allow life to flow.

They give in to the Universe and know that whatever happens is what has to happen and that life takes all the time it needs to allow whatever needs to mature to mature.

They respect the natural process of events.

What do the masters not do?

They do not resist.

They do not control.

They do not complain.

They do not let themselves be overcome by anger.

They do not try to speed up or force things.

They do not live with mistrust.

They do not impose their will or needs on others.

Practice:

Do the exercise described above. Go to a bank, a shop, an office...

Observe yourself and let go.

Finally, express your hope that this meditation will bring benefits to all beings without exception.

Story:

One fine day some Buddhist monks were arguing in the middle of the road. They could not manage to reach an agreement, so they decided to go to the monastery to speak with their master, a well-known lama who was highly respected for his wisdom. The monks went to the wise man's quarters, but they found him meditating and decided to sit outside until he finished.

One hour later the door opened. Both monks stood up and asked the master to act as a judge and, after listening to the two parties, decide who was in the right. The master smiled and invited them to have a tea. After a few minutes of silence, with the cup still in his hands, the wise man asked them to tell him the reason for their dispute.

—I'll speak first —exclaimed one of the monks—, then my companion will speak and, last of all, the master will decide who is right.

The master nodded his head in approval and then the first monk started talking:

—This morning I got up early to go into the village for some medicine. I stopped under a tree to rest for a moment and when I wiped the sweat off my forehead I looked up and saw a butterfly tangled in a spider web, so I decided to free it. Since I couldn't quite reach it, I climbed onto some large clay vessels that were nearby. Unfortunately, right when the butterfly was able to escape, I slipped and the vessels broke. Suddenly, I heard the voice of my friend, the water monk, who was reproaching me for my action. All I have done is free a butterfly from a spider web and I think that I have done nothing wrong. That is all I have to say.

—Ok, now you speak —said the master to the second monk.

—I also got up very early this morning to get water from the well by the tree. The well is very deep and the vessels are not easy to fill. After managing to fill two vessels I sat down for a little while under the tree and I dozed off. I was awakened by a loud noise: my clay vessels had been shattered! And it takes so much effort to fill them up! Now I will have to go to the monastery, get two other vessels, fill them up and take them to the kitchen monk. The water I take to the monastery is more important than a mere butterfly. That is all I have to say.

After a long silence, the master spoke again.

—I do not agree with you —he said to the second monk—. Water is not more important than a butterfly: everything in life, whether it is an animal, a plant, a person or a rock, has its purpose in the universe. I don't agree with freeing a butterfly either, because all the beings I just mentioned have a synchrodestiny, a destiny of synchronized experiences, and you, by freeing the creature, have interfered in it —asserted the master, pointing to the first monk—. Now I am going to tell you both something that you should probably know. A short while ago I spoke with the kitchen monk. He told me that the water monk had not come and that he was very happy. Why? I asked him. He told me that someone had put poison into the well and that if the water monk had brought the water, as he usually does, we would all have been poisoned. Then he told me that the monk in charge of bringing the medicines had not fulfilled his task either but that it was the best thing that could have happened, because the pharmacist had prepared the medicines using the poisoned well water, and if he had brought them, the kitchen monk would now be dead.

So, I will tell you that neither of you are right. But the first monk, by breaking the vessels, saved many lives and the second monk, by arguing about it, avoided the death of the kitchen monk. Everything in life has a meaning, for better or for worse.

The two monks apologized to each other and were glad about everything that had happened, since that day turned out to be a day of happiness because of the good that both of them had done without realizing it.

Álvaro Gutiérrez Castillo

Chapter 19:
Often, the "worst" is the "best" and an accident is a blessing

"Remember that sometimes not getting what you want is a wonderful stroke of luck".

Dalai Lama

Allow me to share two personal experiences that will show very clearly what I mean when I say that whatever happens to us (as bad as it may seem under ordinary perception) is the best thing that could happen, to avoid suffering or to bring us some big blessing or to teach us something.

At the end of the 1990s, I was driving down a road late at night with my girlfriend at the time. We were listening to a cassette tape that we had made of songs that were important to us, songs we had compiled during our relationship of over three years. Suddenly we heard a strange sound and discovered that the tape was getting tangled... By the sound of it the tape was being totally destroyed! To prevent damage to the car's cassette player, which would make matters even worse, I stopped for a moment at a yield sign to extract the yards and yards of tape that were stuck in the machine.

That music had great sentimental value to us and we had but that one copy, we were lamenting to ourselves, when all of a sudden we saw a car flash by, going the wrong way and travelling at an ungodly speed. We froze. It took some time for us to react.

If the tape had not gotten stuck and we had continued along that road, there would have been no way to avoid crashing head-on with that vehicle hurtling along way above the speed limit. And I can assure you, dear friend and reader, that you would not be reading this book right now.

The funny thing is that in the ten years that I owned that car, the cassette player only "failed" that one time.

Here is another example:

In 2003 I took part in an outdoor speed painting competition. We had about five hours to do our paintings and present them to the jury that would choose the lucky winner. If I recall correctly the winner would receive about 700 Euros, a very attractive prize for many of the young painters who were there. Most of us there competing were looking for a way to finance our great passion, and the prize money would go to buying more supplies.

It was a sunny day that made the colorful streets of Gran Canaria look especially beautiful. There was quite a festive ambience on the main street where the event was taking place, thanks to the almost two hundred painters who were working on our paintings with joy and camaraderie.

My intention was to paint the sensations stirred up in me by the island. I started out designing a lovely picture with lots of light and very bright colors, in which red, white and ochre tones formed an oasis of sensations. On that adventure I was accompanied by two friends who had decided to come along to help and keep me company. Both agreed that the painting was one of the best canvasses that I had ever created in that format (100x80cm). And it seems that it did look especially good, according to the comments made by some of the people who started to form a circle around us and were watching with curiosity and expectation.

There were only thirty minutes left before we had to hand in our works when I, quite happy about the work I had done over those past few hours, left the painting on the easel for it to dry. My friends and I looked at it with satisfaction while talking about the sensations that those colors and shapes aroused in us, and we dreamed about a possible victory that would supply my studio with enough canvas, frames and paint to last for months. All of a sudden, to our astonishment, a gust of wind lifted the painting and hurled it to the ground. Our jaws dropped.

My friends threw up their hands and in no time we were surrounded by about fifty people commenting on the tragedy that had befallen that "poor guy". I simply observed the scene in silence, aware of the torrent of reactionary thoughts that were going through my head.

As I picked the painting up off the asphalt I saw the extent of the "pictorial disaster": the canvas was particularly affected in the lower left corner and the upper right corner.

One of my friends stood up and exclaimed: —I'm leaving, this is too painful to watch!

The other one looked at me helplessly and, in an attempt to convey his support, he said, with his head down:

—I'm really sorry, man. I'm here for you.

At least fifteen people came up to me to console me. But one person approached me and stated:

—They say that if an accident occurs during the creation of a work, it is a sign that the work can be improved.

He smiled at me and left. Those words were like an elixir for my heart, so I looked at the painting and asked myself: what is the improvement that it needs? I then began to feel that I should paint two wings that came out of the affected areas and touched in the middle. Something like an angel from the earth and another from the Universe.

I painted it all effortlessly and in record time, before an audience of about a hundred people who watched me, amidst whispers and comments. Just when I went to turn it in, an elderly woman came up to me and exclaimed:

—Wonderful work, young man! It's perfect for my house! How much is it?

I had never sold a painting before so the price I told her was random, but high enough (at least it seemed to me) that she would want to make a counter-offer. But instead the woman said:

—Perfect! I'll take it.

She seemed very pleased and she commissioned me to do another painting. I ended up not winning the contest but the sale of those two paintings brought in a lot more money than the prize would have.

However, for me, the best prize was the experience of overcoming a difficulty. It gave me the confidence I needed to hold, three months later, my first exhibition, which I titled "Inner Beauty" and which was a great success.

Life and the Universe will always push us to give the best of ourselves, and to do so they use their own tools. As Mr. Díaz would often say to me: "Life is always inviting you to dance with her and, with each dance, you become a better dancer".

What do the masters say?

Nothing in life happens by chance, everything has a reason for it, everything is always for our maximum good. It is our resistance to what happens that causes suffering. The greater the resistance, the greater the suffering.

Frequently it seems that things are going badly, or that events are not turning out as we would like. However, when this happens life is inviting us to experience something that connects more deeply with it and with our own essence and true nature.

When you accept and allow things to be as they are, you connect with life and with the joy of living.

It is important to understand that accepting does not mean resignation. To accept and let life flow is not at all like resigning yourself to a painful life that goes against your nature and your freedom. The conflict-oriented mindset can use this tool as a means to justify being mistreated or living a life full of suffering, weighed down by a victim mentality and pain. This is what the masters call "the ego traps," which can mean resigning yourself to pain when life is actually inviting you to experience the opposite: to release, to let go of what is imprisoning you.

Accepting is assuming where you are and taking responsibility for your life.

When we allow life to flow as it is, what at first might appear to be a misfortune or a negative event, always holds within some teaching, blessing or opportunity.

And, to begin, they recommend that you ask yourself: What is the opportunity here? And allow the response to arise from your inner feeling.

Becoming addicted to situations we judge to be positive produces a great deal of suffering, because life is like a piano; we cannot just play the white keys and reject the black keys, we have to integrate the black keys in order to enjoy a lovely, complete symphony.

What do the masters do?

They let things be as they are.

They accept things as they are.

They learn from every situation.

They allow everything to flow, taking responsibility based on consciousness.

They ask their inner self what the teaching or opportunity is in each situation.

They trust fully in life.

They see every situation with eyes of understanding or with the comprehension that comes from their inner self or essence.

What do the masters not do?

They do not resist things as they are. They do not condemn the event. They do not judge the situation.

They do not justify a life of suffering.

They do not use the tool of letting things flow and accepting as an excuse to receive or cause harm, neither in themselves or in other beings.

They do not mistrust life.

They do not feel that they are victims of the circumstances.

Practice:

When you find yourself before a situation that could be considered undesirable, such as an accident, or an unexpected event that causes confusion, stop for a few seconds, or minutes, or whatever time you need. Connect deeply with your inner feeling, draw your attention to your heart and, in communion with it, inhale and state:

"I accept this situation just as it is".

And as you exhale, say:

What is the opportunity here?

At the end of the practice, take a few minutes to observe your feelings in silence and, finally, reaffirm your wish that the benefits of this practice reach all beings without exception.

Story:

"And when do you plan to fulfill your dream?" asked the master of his disciple.
"When I have the opportunity to do so," responded the disciple.
To this the master said: "Opportunity never comes. Opportunity is already here".

Anthony de Mello

Chapter 20:
Changing obligation for opportunity

"Life is an opportunity, not an obligation".

John Heider

In 2004, an extraordinary lama agreed to come to Lanzarote to perform a fascinating ceremony with fire. It was something really worth seeing and I was very interested and eager to attend and receive the lama's blessings. It was going to be held on a Saturday in a lovely house on the outskirts of the city, near Teseguite.

Back then, I worked at the airport. I remember looking at the work schedule with my hours for that month and discovering that precisely that Saturday my shift was from four p.m. to eleven p.m. And the ceremony was from four to ten!

I tried everything: switching shifts with a coworker, asking my supervisor for a day off... But over and over again the answer was an unambiguous no. Something inside me made me feel that I had to go, but at the same time a little voice inside me spoke clearly: "you can't go, you have to work".

That Saturday morning I felt strongly that my place that day was at the lovely house on the outskirts of Teseguite, and not at that noisy airport. So I turned off my cell phone, I unplugged my landline and at 3:30 I went to the place, smiling and saying to myself: "today I can't go to work because I have something important to do".

I spent an incredible afternoon with twenty-five wonderful people. The lama's teachings were amazing: he worked with fire and with the management of emotions. His practices were really effective. I felt calm and peaceful the entire time, knowing that I had made the right decision and that, at the very least, I would have a great story to tell my grandchildren one day.

I arrived home, overflowing with happiness, at around midnight and I went to bed. To make sure that nothing disturbed my big smile, I decided not to turn the phones back on until the next day. When I did so, on Sunday at noon, I saw, to my great surprise, that I had no messages or missed calls. That was a very good sign.

That day, my shift started at three o'clock. As I went in, my coworkers greeted me as usual: "Hello," "How's it going?," "Have a good one"... The things we normally say at such times.

In the office, one of my superiors said hello as he usually did. The other, who had been on duty the day before, spoke to me politely and simply said:

—Hello, José. For yesterday's shift, I'll note down that you took the hours the company owed you for overtime, all right?

I said yes and then we started planning the day's work.

It was an indescribable sensation to feel that I really did do the right thing and that somehow the Universe had harmonized everything so that I could follow the dictates of my heart without any conflict arising as a result.

What do the masters say?

The ideas they transmit in this area are variations on the phrase with which the chapter began: "Life is an opportunity, not an obligation". We tend to set aside what is truly important (health, loved ones, inspirations... our life, in short) for ongoing pressing obligations. In other words, we put urgent activities before important activities.

The word important is comprised of the prefix "in" (interior) and the verb "portar" (to carry), so it can be understood as "that which is carried inside," or that which really offers the benefit of bringing us closer to our inner peace, that which leads us to awakening. In contrast, the word "urgent" can be connected to that external pressure we feel to please people; again, it takes us to the concepts of pleasing others, meeting obligations, fulfilling commitments, obligations...

Forgetting what is truly important and living outside ourselves, viewing life as one big obligation, living without joy: this is one of the biggest poisons created by the conflict-oriented mindset, the origin of "insanity" and a direct access to disease.

What do the masters do?

They seek out opportunities to continue reconnecting with life. They recognize what is important and they give it priority.

They live a revolutionary life, affectionately challenging themselves all the time. They follow their innermost feelings without fear, without worrying about what other people will say.

They live with coherence (moved by Love and Peace, which is our natural state).

They live in freedom.

They walk hand-in-hand with life.

What do the masters not do?

They do not live life as an obligation.

They do not live to please others, but rather with authenticity. They do not forget what is truly important.

They do not go somewhere if their heart is not there. They do not resist opportunities. They do not look for excuses.

They never use the expressions "I have to" or "I must".

Practice:

Stop once in a while. Take a few deep breaths and put your attention on your heart. And ask yourself what obligations are separating you from what really resonates in you, what you truly feel is your purpose in life.

Ask for "inspiration" in finding possible solutions and begin to apply actions leading you to the opportunities given to you by life.

Try to not use the words "I have to" or "I must" for at least seven days. In its place use the expression "It would be worthwhile to..."

Finally, express your hope that this meditation will bring benefits to all beings without exception.

Tibetan blessing:

May all beings be happy.

May all beings find peace.

May all beings be protected from harm, both internal and external.

May all beings be healthy and strong.

May all beings be liberated.

May all beings be enlightened.

So be it.

Chapter 21: Greetings

"Be alert when you speak; with your words you create a world inside you".

Navajo Proverb

One thing that really grabbed my attention about these masters was their way of greeting others. I never heard the typical "Hello," "How's it going?" or "How are you?"

They usually used the expression *namasté*. This word has numerous meanings, all of which are quite similar... Perhaps the one that most resonated in me is the following: "I honor that place in you where the entire universe dwells, that place in you that is a place of light, love and truth. And I know that when you are in that place inside you, and I am in that place inside me, you and I are one.

A shorter version would be: "The Divinity in me sees and honors the Divinity in you". Another one that really drew my attention is: "I greet you with reverence; not you but rather your inner being".

We find similar meanings in the greetings used in other ancestral cultures and philosophies, such as in Hawaii where the expression "aloha" means "in the presence of the divine I greet you".

All of these forms of greeting others or of recognizing the presence of others are certainly an excellent way to connect with the essence of the beings that surround us.

But let's reflect on what happens when we run into somebody and we ask them, using our culture's usual formulas, "How are you?" or "How are things going?"... What we are doing is asking that person to begin pronouncing judgments, by activating his or her dual programs. The answers to these greetings go from "fine" to "horrible" and include "If only you knew..." and they all nourish the role of victim. They are like a direct access icon to duality.

It is also interesting (and very revealing) to examine the responses given by these teachers when they are asked "How are you?":

—Feeling life. —Dancing with life. —Flowing.

—Letting myself be. —Enjoying the moment.

(In silence, allow yourself to simply feel)

Story:

Socrates was famed and respected for his knowledge throughout all of ancient Greece. One day an acquaintance visited the great philosopher and said:

—Do you know what I just heard about your friend?

—Hold on a minute —replied Socrates. Before you say anything, I would like you to do a little test. I call it the triple filter test.

—The triple filter test?

—Correct —continued Socrates—. Before you start telling me about my friend, it might be a good idea to take a moment to filter what you are going to say. That is why I call it the triple filter test. The first filter is the truth: are you absolutely sure that what you are going to say is true?

—No, —said the man—. I actually just heard about it and...

—All right —interrupted Socrates—. So you do not really know if it is true. Now, allow me to apply the second filter, which is that of goodness: is what you are going to tell me about my friend something good?

—No, quite the opposite. You see...

—OK —Socrates went on—, you wish to tell me something bad about my friend and you are not even sure if it is true. You might still pass the test though, because one filter remains; the filter of usefulness. Is what you are going to tell me about my friend useful to me?

—No, I would say that it is not.

—Well then —concluded Socrates—. If what you want to tell me is not true, good or useful, why tell me at all?

Chapter 22: Judgments and prejudices

"What a sad era when it is easier to smash an atom than a prejudice".

Albert Einstein

Now I would like to share two experiences that will help us better understand the influence that judgments and prejudices have on our lives and their tremendous capacity to distort reality.

In the late 1990s, a friend of mine named Arturo was looking for a meditation teacher and he asked me if I knew of anyone. I immediately thought of Ángel, a wonderful person and excellent teacher, one of the first to teach me how to channel energy and how to live in calmness and peace. I gave Arturo his address and, based on my recommendation, he said he would go visit him that very afternoon.

Some time went by before I saw my friend again and had the chance to ask him how the visit had gone. Surprisingly, he told him it had been very disappointing. He had walked away with a very bad impression of Ángel: according to Arturo, he was a terrible teacher who had dedicated barely a few minutes of his time to him. How could he possibly learn mental calm from a person who seemed anxious and sad? His voice trembled when he spoke and it almost seemed that he stuttered! So he decided not to go back.

I found these comments quite baffling. I even thought that we must be talking about different people: perhaps he had made a mistake and gone to visit a different Ángel...

A few months later I happened to run into this teacher at the supermarket. After giving him a big hug and chatting for a few minutes, I asked him if a young man named Arturo had gone to visit him some time ago. He stopped to think for a moment and then remembered a young man who was tall and strong and had blond hair. The description he gave coincided with my friend. What he said next left me speechless. Unfortunately, my teacher had not been able to spend much time with Arturo because when the doorbell rang he was getting ready to leave for the hospital: he had just received a phone call telling him his wife had died.

What most surprised me was that, despite the very painful experience he was going through at that moment, that great person had stopped to spend a few minutes with a complete stranger. But Arturo, knowing nothing of the situation, had judged him and deemed him a "terrible teacher". Here we have a clear example of how our prejudice against another person can cause us to miss good opportunities. Arturo, when he decided not to contact Ángel again, missed the opportunity to learn from one of the greatest Western teachers I have ever met.

The second of the experiences I want to share happened in 2002 during one of my trips to Switzerland. My friends and I were driving to the city after an afternoon of snowboarding. To get there faster we decided to take a shortcut that went through a village. My friends were in a hurry because they wanted to get to the city before nightfall but, as we drove into town, we ran into a circus parade in which dozens of clowns, acrobats, puppeteers and all sorts of animals were marching down the street, making it quite difficult to get through. We were soon trapped in the middle of the hullaballoo and had no choice but to follow the parade. We were right behind an elephant, from which we tried to keep a safe distance. However, at one point we got too close. Imagine our surprise when that immense animal sat down on the hood of our car! There we were, the five occupants of the car, contemplating in astonishment the scene as if it were a surrealist film. Jeff got out of the driver's seat and in a state of indignation started looking for the event organizer. When the rest of us could finally react, we got out of the car and tried to calm him down. It would serve no purpose to complain because the truth was that we were responsible because we had gotten too close to the animal.

It turns out that Jeff was a mechanic specialized in bodywork and paint and he soon saw that we could relax. Apart from the huge dent, the car had suffered no damage, so we decided to get on the freeway at the next entrance. We were about to get on the freeway when we saw a police checkpoint. When they saw the state of the car one of the agents indicated that we should pull over. In Switzerland cars with any type of damage, even dents, are not allowed on the road.

Jeff stopped and rolled down the window. The police officer walked up to the car and started reproaching us harshly for driving a car in such a state of repair, reciting the chapter, the article and practically the paragraph of the traffic law that said that doing so was prohibited.

—I apologize, officer. What happened is that an elephant sat down on the hood —was the only thing that good old Jeff could think of to offer as an explanation.

I must admit that the rest of the car's occupants did nothing to improve the situation, because we all burst into laughter, finding it impossible to repress it in such absurd circumstances.

The officer quickly called a fellow officer and they performed a breath test on Jeff. The result was negative but the five of us couldn't stop laughing, so they decided to also test him for drugs. They must have thought that we were all under the effects of some hallucinatory substance! When they saw that the drug test also came back negative, they called the village authorities to check out our story and they confirmed that an elephant had in fact sat on the hood of our car. Two hours and thirty minutes later, after speaking with a couple of police stations and even with the mayor (they did everything but call the President) they allowed us to go, with no charges and no fine.

It is very interesting to see how we sometimes find ourselves in situations that are difficult to understand or believe if we observe them from the perspective of our judgments, limitations and prejudices.

What do the masters say?

We identify very closely with our opinions, judgments and beliefs, and this prevents us from seeing reality as it is and means that we are only capable of perceiving our interpretations of that reality.

We condition our perception of life with our memories, resistances and judgments (our conflict-oriented mindsets or ego) to such a degree that we constantly miss great opportunities in this life.

The word karma means "action". So, for these great masters, "liberation" means "being free of all action" or ceasing to be slaves and acting in a reactionary way according to our filters based on fear and separation.

We are constantly acting and, because of our lack of trust, we try to control things or force life to go where we think it should, to fit our preferences. Similarly, we condition our mind, inducing it to believe only what matches our conflict-oriented mindsets. Thus we end up reducing what life really is and who we really are.

There are people who, taking on the role of "world organizer" or "executive director of the universe," would even prefer to get sick rather than let go of resistances and allow life to be as it is.

All the masters agree that reality distortion and suffering appear when we apply memory to the present moment.

What do the masters do?

They observe everything as it is. They see life without filters.

They start the day with new eyes (unfettered by memory).

They listen and observe like a child (unfettered by beliefs).

They let go of judgments and prejudices.

They perceive people without their past.

They have a neutral and innocent attitude in every event or situation.

They live in inspiration, not in memory.

They let things be as they are.

They choose to perceive with love.

What do the masters not do?

They do not condition things with their judgments, beliefs or expectations.

They do not apply memory to the present.

They do not resist things as they are.

They do not use criticism or sarcasm.

They do not perceive with fear and mistrust.

They do not allow their memories to interpret reality.

Practice:

Every morning, when you wake up, put your attention on your heart and make the following affirmations, feeling the emotion:

"With total acceptance and joy, I begin this day with new eyes.

I will let go of control and will not allow my memories to be my guide today; in its place I will choose love.

Choosing peace will be my only alternative,

and returning to my inner self or essence will be my only aim, in benefit of all beings without exception.

Thank you, thank you, thank you!"

Story:

While he was on his morning walk around the monastery, a lama found an 8-year-old monk crying in front of a spider web.

—Why are you crying little one? —the lama asked him.

—I am crying because I saw a little fly fall into this spider web... And the spider killed it.

—I see... But who are you crying for? For the fly or for the spider?

—For the fly, of course! — responded the young monk.

—But in fact —said the lama— the one you should really be crying for is the spider. The fly has been busy moving, exploring and experiencing various places and situations before dying. In contrast, the spider spends its entire life stuck in the same place, always doing the same thing, waiting for its food.

And the child started to smile while his heart grew bigger.

Chapter 23: Ironies of destiny

"*A person often meets his destiny on the road he took to avoid it*".

Jean de La Fontaine

"*Until you make the unconscious conscious,
it will direct your life and you will call it fate*".

Carl G. Jung

My beloved older sister got pregnant at the age of 21: it came as a big surprise to her, bringing uncertainty and confusion. I remember that when she told me she was upset and did not know what to do. I tried to calm her down and I advised her to tell our parents, in the best way possible: for them it was sure to be a tremendous shock.

She was very worried. She spoke with various people about it, including an older cousin of ours who recommended that she have an abortion: she was very young and to have a child at that age could ruin her career and her life. My sister ruled out that idea but four years later something happened that made me remember that cousin's advice.

My nephew had already turned three when one day, at a family gathering, all the cousins got together to play a game of basketball. Even though he was the smallest, David ran fast and he moved easily among us. At one point he tried to get the ball away from the cousin who had scared my sister with the idea that she would ruin her life if she decided to have that little tadpole. Holding the ball between his hands, the boy looked at my cousin closely and asked him with a somewhat derisive tone:

—And what's your name?

When he heard the name, he laughed out loud and exclaimed: —That's not a very nice name!

How ironic! Four years ago, someone advised my sister to have an abortion and now, the child was before him, stealing the ball and laughing at his name.

The most interesting thing about this case was what happened when my nephew was 16 years old. We were at a café having a snack when this cousin came in, said hello to us and went to sit with some friends at a table on the other side of the bar. I decided that it was a good time to tell my nephew the story. His reaction was typical of a person that age. He became very angry and said something like "I'm going over there to tell him that it's his mother who should have had an abortion". I quickly put my hand on his shoulder and advised him not to let himself be carried away by that reaction.

—Let's think about this, David: if you had a friend that age who told you she had gotten pregnant without wanting to, what would you tell her? Think about it. You don't have to say it out loud. Whatever you decide to tell her, I'm sure you would say it with the idea of trying to help her and not of hurting the child. Right?

David went quiet for a moment, observing his emotions, and then he said:

—Well then, what I really have to do then is say thank you to my mother for not taking his advice.

And after that he just smiled and drank some more orange juice.

(In silence, allow yourself to simply feel)

Ancient Mayan prayer

Great Creator, Heart of the Sky and the Earth —you made us;
we give you thanks for having created us.
God of thunder, God of rain:
Starting every sunrise we search for peace this world over.

May there be freedom, serenity, and health for all people—
for your children who live to the East, where the sun rises.

We also ask, at the setting of the sun in the West,
that all suffering, pain, and all anger, end —just as the day is ending, too.

That your light may illuminate the thoughts and the lives of those who shed tears,
those who are oppressed, those who have not heard...

And we pray toward the South, where the Heart of the Sea purifies all that is
corrupt, ill, or pestilent.
Give us fortitude so that our voices may reach you —heart, hands, feet.
Before you we kneel with our offerings; we invoke you day and night.

And we turn toward the North and pray, trusting that the Heart of the Wind
will carry to your ears the voices and the cries of your children.

Oh Great Creator —Heart of both Sky and Earth (Our Mother):
give us Life, much of it, and give us a useful existence so that all villages may find
peace in every nation of the world.

Chapter 24:
The lama and the haunted house

"Shadow does not exist: What you call shadow is the light you cannot yet see".

Henri Barbusse

In August of 2002 a Tibetan Buddhist lama agreed to come to Lanzarote to teach a week-long course. Because it was high season on the island, the organizers were having difficulty finding accommodations for him, so one of them suggested an old house that was in Villa de Teguise. The others did not like the idea much, because everyone in Villa de Teguise knew that the house was "haunted". Many ghost stories were told about that place. In fact, the number of paranormal events experienced by the people who had lived there was so high that the case had even been studied by a group of parapsychologists.

However, since it was quite impossible to find any other accommodations for him and since a Tibetan Buddhist lama was not likely to believe in superstitions and nonsense of that sort, they decided to lodge him there. When the time came, they went to the airport to pick him up, they drove him to the door of the house and they gave him the keys, saying only that they would pick him up at 9 the next morning. The lama thanked them and went inside.

The next day everybody wanted to know how the lama's night had been. However, nobody dared ask him. On the first day, the lama's attitude revealed nothing unusual: in fact, he taught his course with total normality and in absolute calm. By the third day, one of the organizers could not hold it in anymore and during one of the meals, she asked him about it, like this:

—There is something I want to ask you. I know it's silly but... some people say that the house you are staying in is haunted...

So I wanted to ask if you had noticed anything unusual during your time there.

He looked at her and simply said: —Ah! So that's the reason...

And he continued eating his soup.

She, of course, wanted to know more, so she asked for details about his experience.

—On the first day —said the lama— when I went in the house, I heard some loud noises coming from the kitchen, so I thought that, with such a large house, there must be someone in charge of maintenance. But when I got to the kitchen, it was empty. I went to my room and, again, I heard the noises. If I went to the bathroom, I heard noises in the hallway and, while I was sleeping, it was as if someone were touching my face. I realized that something was going on. So I got up, lit some incense and put some flowers in a vase. I offered them to those beings with all my love and the "strange" activity stopped.

By sending them love, these beings, which are nothing but residual psychological energy that feeds off fear and resistance, stopped interfering. So, here we have another example of how, by acting with love, we can harmonize even the place in which we happen to be.

(In silence, allow yourself to simply feel)

Story:

While the teacher was giving class to his students, a black ink stain fell onto the white paper on which he was writing. He asked his students:

—What do you see?

And they all answered at the same time:

—A black stain

The teacher responded:

—All of you have noticed the black stain. None of you has seen the rest of the white page, which is much larger.

Chapter 25:
Changing the world with your smile (and not letting the world change your smile)

"The revolution of love begins with a smile. Smile five times a day at someone you would rather not smile at. You must do it for peace".

Mother Teresa of Calcutta

"Be the change you want to see in the world".

Mahatma Gandhi

In the early 2000s, a good friend of mine invited me to spend a few days with him at his house, so I had the chance to fly to Russia and visit Moscow. We used mainly the metro to get around and there I discovered something that really surprised me: nobody smiled.

I remember one day on which we were riding in the last car of the train. I was very happy to be on vacation, to have the chance to see so many things that were new to me, to spend time with my friend after so long. These sensations naturally put a big smile on my face.

Suddenly, someone stood up and started walking towards us. When he had come close, he said something in Russian, and my friend nodded in response.

—He asked for you to please stop smiling. You make them uncomfortable —he explained—. Maybe they think you are laughing at them...

When I heard this I nodded and said: —No problem!

I calmly turned to face the car's rear window, putting my back to the rest of the passengers and I continued to smile as I looked through the glass. I was sure about one thing; I wasn't about to stop expressing my happiness.

Another interesting case about this topic happened to me a few years ago. It was the day that Andrés came to my office for the first time. When the doorbell rang, I went to the door and opened it with a big welcoming smile on my face.

—Good morning, Andrés, how are you? —I asked him as we shook hands.

—Well, here I am, struggling as usual... More of the same old crap— he responded with a serious, preoccupied expression.

—Well, well... Tell me about that! How can I help you? —I inquired with a big smile, as he sat down.

—I have cancer and the doctor says I have three months to live —he answered, this time with an even more serious expression, with a face that seemed to reveal a deep anguish.

There was a brief silence during which Andrés looked at me uncomfortably, until he spat out the following words:

—And what are you laughing at!

I simply kept smiling and I answered him calmly:

—At those doctor's faces when, in the space of a year or two, you are healthier than they are.

Andrés burst into laughter.

—Wow! Now that's optimism; everything else is child's play! I like it!

In about seven months, Andrés had cured his cancer completely, thanks to the changes he made in his mental patterns and the elimination of the rancor he had accumulated.

(In silence, allow yourself to simply feel)

Poem:

"*All thoughts, good and bad,*
that come from my mind cause hardly a ripple,
because their action is as false
as the moon's reflection on the sea".

Tibetan Buddhist meditation poem

Chapter 26: Something unexpected

"Life is like a box of chocolates, you never know what you're gonna get".

Forrest Gump

I remember a lovely winter day about 15 years ago, when I went surfing with two friends in a fantastic spot called Caletón Blanco, in the northern part of the island.

After surfing an amazing wave that had brought me many marvelous sensations, I returned to the line up and was surprised to see my two friends rowing as fast as they could to a nearby reef that was exposed during low tide. They scrambled onto the solid mass, pulling their boards out of the water as if the devil were on their tail, and at the same time they pointed at the water and shouted things that I, from my position, couldn't manage to hear: they seemed to be quite agitated! I kept smiling at the waves while my friends shouted and waved their arms. I moved towards them and, as soon as I was a bit closer, I heard the word "shark".

I barely had time to react. Right at that very moment I saw a fin sticking about 40 cm out of the water, moving towards me at high speed. I still remember it clearly: the fin submerged when it reached me and I felt something pass underneath my surfboard. I automatically lifted my arms and legs while feeling a tremendous shiver going through my entire body, followed by a cold sweat. For an instant I saw nothing. A minute later, the fin appeared again, moving towards me at top speed. I felt my heart about to explode. My legs were almost paralyzed and my breath was faltering; only seconds passed but they seemed like an eternity.

Again, the animal went just under my board, while I raised my legs. This time I noticed that it stopped under me and looking down I could make out a dark gray shape moving in semicircles below me.

Then, about five meters ahead of me a majestic dolphin broke the silence with a spectacular jump. After recovering my normal breathing and heart rate, I started to laugh, thrilled by the beauty of the situation. I could hardly believe it. The dolphin started doing little somersaults around me. What a huge gift this marvelous ocean was giving me! After about fifteen minutes, the dolphin decided to move on to different waters. All I could do was express my amazement and gratitude to the Universe for such a magnificent offering. In the meantime my friends were applauding from the reef.

How interesting that what I first perceived as a threat turned out actually to be a great joy!

(In silence, allow yourself to simply feel)

Story:

One time the Dalai Lama was asked what he found most surprising about humanity. This is what he said:

—Man. Because he sacrifices his health in order to make money. Then he sacrifices money to recuperate his health. And then he is so anxious about the future that he does not enjoy the present; the result being that he does not live in the present or the future; he lives as if he is never going to die, and then dies having never really lived.

Chapter 27: Money is neutral

"Money is a good servant but a bad master".

Alexandre Dumas

"The richest man is not he who has the most, but he who needs the least".

Buddha

At the beginning of the year 2000 I bought some lottery tickets along with some workmates. The grand prize was quite succulent and that afternoon we were fantasizing about what we would do with the money if we won. We are alone in the office, or at least that's what we thought.

—I —exclaimed one of my co-workers enthusiastically— would use the money to remodel my house and to travel around the world , to see all those places that I've always dreamed about. And I would donate money to a NGO so they could build a hospital or a school in some needy part of the planet.

—Well, as for me —exclaimed the other one, pointing at the runway and gesturing grandiosely— the first thing I would do would be to build a giant articulated doll that I would place facing the boss's window... Here, how about this... Every thirty seconds it would give him the finger and tell him "Go to hell!"

He went on like this for a while, delighting in the story. At one point, the boss, who had heard the first part of the conversation but then left, came back into the office to pick up something he had forgotten. But my co-worker was so absorbed in his show that he didn't notice his presence:

—And then I would pull down my pants and pee all over the place: tables, papers, computers...

Since this book is intended to contribute to people's harmony and well-being, I will not reproduce here the long list of insults that came from the mouth of this person who now was about to lose his job. Suffice it to say that his jaw dropped to the floor when he turned around and found the boss, who asked him politely to accompany him inside his office for a moment.

Here we have a clear example of how money is neutral: it is the person in question that allows money to bring out the best or the worst in us.

What do the masters say?

Money is energy and therefore it is neutral. It simply connects with your perception and emotion regarding it. If you fight this energy, it will not come to you and if you love the energy, it will seek you out.

In the words of Mr. Díaz: "Money is not toxic, what is toxic are your beliefs about it".

They understand that the issue of money creates considerable controversy, due to the dysfunctional beliefs that we have absorbed, which come from our culture, family and even religion.

If you think that money is bad, it will not come into your life; if you think it is something that can help you and others grow, that can help you move forward and contribute valuable things to this world, it will come in great abundance.

They say that money does not bring happiness. But neither does poverty! In truth, nothing outside of you can make you really happy.

Money can act as a trigger, either because of its excess or its scarcity, of the emotional poverty or wealth that can exist within you.

The masters understand that life gives you what you are, not what you desire.

If you are already happy, abundance comes naturally and fluidly, because your natural state is joy, abundance, gratitude, love. If you are unhappy (or to put it a better way, if you are generating unhappiness for yourself) and you hope that money or something external will give you happiness, your life will be filled with suffering and you will travel down a river of dissatisfaction. If you are ill at ease with money it will never come to you, or if it does, it will be after great effort and only briefly.

The most important thing is to keep in mind that your true nature is abundant: it is not lacking anything. If you can feel this abundance despite the external circumstances, you will be truly happy and prosperous and, consequently, as a reflection of your inner state, prosperity and abundance will come to you by themselves.

If we consider money to be an end in itself, with the idea of having it just for the sake of having it, to show it off or even to create a personality or identity based on money, we start to feel that we are in disharmony with the world and with ourselves: we are dissatisfied, because in truth money is just a means. A means that can allow us, for example, to have the financial freedom to travel, to exchange knowledge, to learn...

An excellent idea that many masters speak of is that of "money with a conscience," which is money acquired without exploiting other beings or the planet itself, without mistreating nature, money that contributes added value, increased awareness and growth to the world.

Another interesting vision is that of "happy money". In one of his books, Robert G. Allen looks at this issue and tells a funny story: while he was in India, he was approached by a little girl aged about seven, who said this to him:

—Sir, could you give me some happy money?

—Excuse me? What do you mean by "happy money"? —he asked in surprise.

—It's very easy: give me the amount that makes you happy... and it will make me happy too!

What do the masters do?

They understand and accept the fact that the world's means of exchange is money, although they know that this will change some day and we will find other means of exchange.

They relate to this energy with acceptance, joy and love.

They feel abundant and money comes into their lives naturally and without effort.

They share their abundance.

They let money bring out the best in them.

They treat it as a means with which to obtain financial freedom. They contribute many good things to the world with their money.

What do the masters not do?

They do not consider money an end in itself but rather a means. They have no need for money.

They do not resist financial abundance.

They are not ill at ease with money (or with anything else in life). They do not have limiting beliefs regarding it.

They do not become corrupt for money or for anything else.

They do not fall into the limiting and dysfunctional belief that being spiritual means being against money.

They do not create an identity based on money or on anything outside of themselves.

Prosperity practice:

Early in the morning, right when you get out of bed, stretch your arms out to the sides and make the following affirmations:

As you inhale: "I allow all the abundance of the Universe to flow through me".

As you exhale: "I free myself of my resistance".

As you inhale: "I allow myself to be happy and prosperous".

As you exhale: "I release all of my limitations". "Thank you, thank you, thank you!"

Finally, express your hope that this meditation will bring benefits to all beings without exception.

Story:

—Hey, how come you are in such good health? —Because I never argue.

—Oh, that can't be the reason!

—Ok, maybe that isn't the reason!

Chapter 28:
The two entrepreneurs and love

"Before going out in search of revenge, dig two graves".

Confucius

"An eye for an eye makes the whole world blind".

Mahatma Gandhi

Jaime and Luis were two good friends who had decided to embark together on an entrepreneurial adventure. The situation in the country, the much-feared economic crisis that everyone was talking about, made them both nervous that their business might lose money or even fail entirely. It didn't take long for the result of this attitude to appear and their fears soon materialized. The company had to close, which generated considerable distress in both men and led to their relationship degenerating quickly. A series of accusations began in which each blamed the other for the company going bust, and they went so far as hiring lawyers and taking legal action.

After several months of conflict, Jaime came to my office early one morning. He told me he felt terrible about the situation. That afternoon he had to meet with his old partner and friend, Luis, to make some important decisions and work out all the claims that had been filed. Also, he was very anxious because Luis was asking for 80% of the capital invested, to make up, Luis said, for his ex-partner's incompetence.

So, after weeks of insomnia and a severe headache that wouldn't go away, Jaime had very little strength left and he asked me desperately for a solution, advice, anything...

—Love that person. Feel love for him —I advised him.

—I'm afraid those hippy ideas aren't my thing. All that love and stuff is fine for other areas of life, but here we are talking about the business world... Love and business do not go together.

—That's it precisely. But love applies to all spheres, because love is life, growth, expansion, prosperity. So if you don't apply love to what you do, whatever that may be, it won't work.

—But I feel incredible anger and resentment towards him. I simply can't love him —insisted Jaime.

—What you do is just visualize and imagine him during the day today as if he were very happy, as if all of his dreams and expectations were coming true. Think about him as a person who travels around the world, who is doing well, who is fulfilling his dreams, who is happy.

—All right. That's something I can do. At the very least I get to do something other than spend the whole day preoccupied and full of anguish, thinking about awful things.

It was past eleven when I received a call from Jaime who was euphoric and still in shock from what had happened: at the scheduled time he had entered the room where the meeting was to be held, expecting to find a Luis showing signs of anger and rejection. However, Luis stood up smiling, put his hand on his old friend's shoulder, and said:

—Jaime: all day long I have been thinking about our situation and about what has brought us here. I've realized that it wasn't fair for me to try to keep more money than is rightfully mine. In truth, you are not at fault for the company's failure...at least not any more than I am. So I have decided that I am going to withdraw all my claims. I am really sorry that we, after being such good friends, have reached this point... I can only hope that we are capable of working it out a different way.

After saying that, he apologized and gave him a big hug. For the first time ever they cried together and then they started recalling the good times they had shared in the past.

Even though he was directly involved in this story, Jaime could hardly believe what had just happened. Actually, it is quite simple: he had stopped feeding and giving energy to that conflict, to instead generate love and reconnect with his friend's heart.

Practice:

Do the exercise described in the story above, focusing on someone with whom you currently have a conflict. Do it several times a day for at least seven days.

Finally, express your hope that this meditation will bring benefits to all beings without exception.

Reflection:

Two people have been living in you all your life. One is the ego, garrulous, demanding, hysterical and calculating; the other is the hidden spiritual being, whose quiet voice of wisdom you have only rarely heard or attended to. As you listen more and more to the teachings, contemplate them and integrate them into your life, your inner voice, your innate wisdom of discernment, what in Buddhism we call "discriminating awareness" is awakened and strengthened, and you begin to distinguish between its guidance and the various clamorous and enthralling voices of the ego. The memory of your real nature, with all its splendor and confidence, begins to return to you. You will find, in fact, that you have uncovered in yourself your own wise guide.

Rinpoche, Sogyal: The Tibetan Book of Living and Dying

Chapter 29: Intuition (internal tutor)

"True intuition opens the doors to truth. If we want to continue using the word intuition we have to forget that it refers to instinct, and that it is sometimes attributed to women, I don't know why, since intelligence is not at all related to one's sex".

Consuelo Martín, philosopher

It is very important to always follow our inner voice, that part of us that whispers to us from the heart and, through our feelings, invites us to take the path of peace and to avoid suffering.

In the year 2003 something happened to me that illustrates how intuition works: my girlfriend at the time was set to arrive at the airport after a long trip and I had bought her a lovely bouquet of roses. To keep them looking nice, I decided to go to the city and buy a vase for them. I drove around looking for a place to park until I found a street that had quite a few spaces and I started the necessary maneuvers. But something inside me was telling me not to park there. It was a strong feeling and I had it for quite some time: even when I had gotten out of the car and was walking away, I kept feeling that I should go back and put the car somewhere else. My rational mind, exercising its function of voiding or questioning how I felt inside, decided that all of that was nonsense. Also, I didn't have much time (the programmed mind always makes references to time and is usually in a hurry). So I quickly walked to a shop in which I found a beautiful Japanese vase that would look fantastic with those 21 red roses. With that image in my mind, I went back to where I had parked the car. To my great surprise I saw that someone had forced the lock! Someone had broken into my car to steal... the bouquet of roses!

In ten minutes I had to be at the airport, so I had no time to buy more flowers. So I gave my girlfriend a beautiful Japanese vase... with nothing in it. The expression on her face when I told her the story gave me the impression that she didn't entirely believe me, something she confirmed years later.

Another example of how important it is to pay attention to this voice or inner guide is what happened to me on my trip to Moscow (which I talked about earlier, in Chapter 25). I was with some friends on the subway platform, about to get on a train, when I noticed a man who seemed very nervous and kept looking at me. I had a strong sensation: that agitated young man had some sort of hostile intention. When the train stopped and opened its doors, I saw the person getting on the train before us and looking at us out of the corner of his eyes. I was about to ask my friends to change to a different car, something inside me was whispering for me to do it. But I decided to ignore that "something". I didn't want to inconvenience my friends, plus, they would think I was paranoid.

We stepped into the car. When the train started moving, the young man came up to me. He showed me a police badge and asked me to show him my passport. I did so. After looking at it, he told me there was a problem with the passport and that I had to accompany him, by myself. My friends, who were all Russian, asked him again and again what the problem was. He didn't answer. He just said that it had a problem and that I had to go with him. My friends were beginning to be suspicious of the strange behavior of that police officer dressed as a civilian, so they told him that first we would go to a police station located in the metro station to check if he really was a police officer. When we got there, it turned out that he wasn't. The real agents arrested the impostor: they explained that it was a plot used to swindle people. In Russia, at least back then, people were not allowed to be on the streets without their passport and that young man acted like a police officer so that he could get his hands on my passport. To get it back, I would have had to pay him (they usually asked for about 300 dollars). passport. To get it back, I would have had to pay him (they usually asked for about 300 dollars).

My friends and I left in a calm state of mind and decided to take this strange story as a mere anecdote: there was no reason to make a big deal out of it.

A few days later, no more than three, I was with Viktor, one of my Russian friends, going back to the house where we were staying. It was about 11 p.m. and we were about four blocks away from our destination. All of a sudden, we were assaulted by five individuals dressed in black and carrying clubs. They didn't need to say a word: it was clear that their intention was to beat us up. One of them tried to hit my head, but "intuitively" I crouched down, thus avoiding the blow. My friend, who was a great athlete and no doubt could have left me far behind in the blink of an eye, shouted at me: "Run!" So I took off as fast as I could, with two of the thugs just behind me. When I reached the house an elderly woman who had seen me around over the past week opened the door for me. I went up to the house and waited for my friend, who got there half an hour later with various injuries.

The police found out that the group that had assaulted us lived just three buildings down from the house in which we were staying. They had been hired by that fake police officer. It seems he wanted to get revenge on us for taking him to the police station that day.

I returned to Spain a few days later having learned a great lesson: always pay attention to the voice or inner guide that is our intuition, a word that comes from "in" and "tutor" or teacher; that is, our "inner teacher".

(In silence, allow yourself to simply feel)

Story:

One night a man heard someone moving around in his house. He got out of bed and, because it was pitch dark, he tried to make sparks with the flint, so that he could light his lamp.

But the thief who had made the noise came and stood in front of him and every time that a spark touched the lamp's wick, he discretely put it out with his finger. The man, believing that the wick was wet, never saw the thief.

In your heart there is also someone who is putting out the fire without you seeing him.

Rumi

Chapter 30: The ego and its mental program of conflict and suffering

"Descartes said: 'I think, therefore I am.' But, from the perspective of Buddha's teachings, we could say: "I think, therefore I am... not here".

Thich Nhat Hanh

"Like the fate of a fragile bubble, try as we might to defend a separate mentality and to identify with our image, being part of the unity (of the whole) is inevitable".

Kalu T.

At this point in the book I would like to briefly explain some key ideas that will help us better understand all the chapters and, especially, the language of the teachers who reflect on the main topic of each of the stories.

As you progress through this book, you will find the following reflection a number of times: "happiness is already inside us, but we have set up barriers or obstacles that separate us from it". Let's look at exactly what it is that prevents us from enjoying what we already have.

I will begin with this illustrative extract about the Buddha's illumination, which is found in Gueshe Kelsang Gyatso's book *"Introduction to Buddhism"*:

"As dusk fell, Devaputra Mara, the chief of all the demons, or *maras*, in this world, tried to disturb Siddhartha's concentration by conjuring up many fearful apparitions. He manifested hosts of terrifying demons: some throwing spears, some firing arrows, some trying to burn him with fire, and some hurling boulders and even whole mountains at him...

However, Siddhartha remained imperturbable. Through the force of his concentration, the raging fires became like offerings of rainbow lights and the weapons, rocks, and mountains appeared to him as a rain of fragrant flowers...In this way he triumphed over all the demons of this world, which is why he subsequently became known as "Conqueror Buddha".

In Buddhist philosophy, the concept of *mara* represents the mental contaminations that we all have, an identity that is separate, created... It is the same as what we might call "ignorance" and it is what prevents beings from awakening or discovering their true nature. In Buddhist texts it is represented as a kind of dark deity but in fact it is nothing but our mental constructions based on fear, attachment and memories with which we are completely identified (the ego).

This representation of *mara* has received many names by different masters: ego, conflict-oriented mindset, separate mind, reactionary mind, conceptual mind, darkness, erroneous perception (based on fear), false identity and other more modern descriptions (for example, once I heard Richard Brodie, the author of "*Virus of the mind*" refer to it as mental programming; Sogyal Rinpoche has called the ego "the character" that we have built and with which we identify). In this case, I will refer to it as conflict-oriented programming or mental program.

The Spanish philosopher and writer Consuelo Martín, making use of the same terminology, offers a masterly definition of what I am referring to with this reflection: "*As long as I trust mental programming to discover the truth, I will not be free. I depend on thought-based interpretations. Could I see that this function that is represented mentally and to which we all contribute with our beliefs is not reality?*"

Now, allow me to put forward some general ideas that will help us to better understand what we are referring to when talking about the ego and its conflict-oriented mental programs or the reactionary mind, concepts that we are looking at in a specific and practical way through the stories presented in this book.

The ego is what you believe you are: personality, taste, judgments, memories, beliefs, fears, culture, education... It is a system made up of thoughts that defend this structure, imposing it on life and on truth. A very limited and long-suffering version of yourself and one that is, above all else, false. This is what the teachers call ignorance, what separates you from your self and from truth. To live free of the suffering caused by this mental programming is what Buddhists call reaching *nirvana* (absence of affliction).

One of the main goals of the ego and its reactionary mental program is to defend this structure that we have created and with which we identify; therefore, it reacts with attacks and defenses, because it is based on fear. So, instead of living we subsist, we behave as if we were mere survivors, mistrusting, controlling and in constant opposition with what we really are: Love and Peace.

This is what was attacking Buddha in the metaphor used in the preceding text (...some threw spears and arrows, some tried to burn him with fire, and some hurled boulders and even whole mountains) and it is attacking you as well: it is nothing but a structure of reactionary thoughts that are there to defend (through fear and attacks) the "indiviDUAL" identity (separate mind) with which we have identified ourselves.

Siddhartha, like other great masters, discovers that he is not part of that identity, and he dissociates from it, breaking the bars that imprisoned him in this mental program. He thus awakens and ceases to be a slave to these programs or reactionary systems, and he returns to the "UNItary" mind (unity); and for this reason he is given the name Buddha (the awakened one).

Now, how does this web of ego and its conflict-oriented systems come into being? The ego forms part of a field of thoughts and memory from the collective unconscious mind and it is born from an initial thought of separation. Believing that we are separate, we compete, we judge, we feel that we are in need, we struggle and we experience fear. These references appear in the metaphor used in the story of Adam and Eve, who lived in Paradise (unity) and were expelled from it for eating from the tree of good and evil (duality); at that point guilt appears and they fall into a deep sleep: *"From any tree of the garden you may eat freely; but from the tree of the knowledge of good and evil you shall not eat, for in the day that you eat from it you will surely die"*. (Genesis 2, 16-17).

For this reason many great masters call those who are totally identified with the ego's mental program (separate entity) "the living dead" and, similarly, they describe the process of discovering the true nature of the self as "coming back to life".

This separate identity system is so fully integrated that we have taken it upon ourselves to defend it and transmit it to future generations. Notice, for example, how babies come into this world full of innocence and completely connected with their essence. They feel unlimited and have unconditional love for themselves and for the beings around them. They are like a mirror that reflects everything as it really is, with innocent perception.

However, as children grow, their parents, their family, society, schools, etc. teach them fears and separation. This makes them conditioned; it is as if we were installing "programs" in their minds which, from this point forward, disconnect them, at a number of levels, from how things really are: love, full acceptance, innocence, gratitude, freedom and the present moment in a pure state.

A child's priority thus becomes pleasing others, being valued by others, living a life based on image, being loved and accepted... The child will fear failure, but he or she will also fear success, and will also fear death and being alone... The child will search for happiness outside of him or herself. It may happen that the need to be different or special pushes the child to become something that he or she really is not.

Clearly, the ego is our idea of what we are and of what the world is, like a kind of filter that distorts our perception, coloring and conditioning reality. This means that instead of experiencing life and truth, we experience interpretations and opinions about it; interpretations and opinions based on our fears, addictions, memories... This filter is conditioned by our whole system of beliefs, judgments, attachments, education, past experiences, etc. And all of this disconnects us from our true nature and essence. The primary function of the ego is to keep us distracted, disconnected from how we feel and out of the present moment. It tries to keep us either in the past, with feelings of guilt, or in the future, filling us with fear in the form of worries.

Another one of its functions is to ensure that we always stay the same and that nothing changes, because its initial aim is to give us "security" in what is really an impermanent world. And upon this ego we have built a personality, the sole purpose of which is to provide us with a false sensation of safety and immutability, in a world that is constantly changing. It is interesting, and also very revealing, to note that the word "personality," which comes from the Greek, means "mask" in this language.

Many of you will be familiar with a phase we were often told in childhood: "Get out there and become someone". And that someone you turn into is not you, but rather someone that others would like, an image adopted to please others.

I recall a funny thing that happened when my nephew David was four. A woman came up to him and said:

—Oh, what a beautiful child! What are you going to be when you grow up?

The boy, feeling disconcerted, looked at me and then back at the woman. Then he touched his heart for a moment and exclaimed:

—Huh? Am I going to be something else? I don't want to be something else! I want to be me!

This is the spontaneous response of a little master! Curiously enough, when I have shared this anecdote, other people have told me that they too have heard answers like this one, from many children who do not want to be "something else," and in a number of different countries. This is evidence that children live in connection with what they really are, as we have seen in some earlier chapters.

The great masters define ego as false identity, as full identification with our maelstrom of thoughts that indicate we are separate from the rest and that are fed by fear, guilt, defense, attachment and attack. It makes us run around outside of ourselves, looking elsewhere for what we already have within us. We run like a donkey with a carrot hanging in front of him, but attached to a stick: run as we might, we will never reach it, since the ego's mantra is "search and never find".

Sometimes, personal growth teachers and coaches call this frenzy for searching outside of oneself "the rat race": it is as if we were in a cage, running on a hamster treadmill, thinking that we are moving forward but without really moving an inch from our original place.

In the words of the great master Sogyal Rinpoche: "When your amnesia over your identity begins to be cured, you will realize that all that grasping at self is the root cause of all suffering. You will understand at last how much harm it has done both to yourself and to others".

The ego and its conflict-oriented mental programs question everything, to make sure that nothing changes; this is why some masters define it as "the barrier that you yourself put in front of you and that separates you from life". Some more of the ego's mantras are:

Careful!

And what if...?

Yes, but...

Whatever you do it will not be enough...

I can't...

That is impossible...

I already know that...

Seek and you won't find...

I am no good at this...

I am special...

I am not as good as...

I am better than...

But the good news is that at every instant, regardless of your past or where you are now, you can choose to live life as a pure life without limits (your Essence), or as a separate object, limited and with its history of itself (Ego).

Practice:

In a quiet place, take a few deep breaths, and as you exhale release all your tension and even your expectations.

Connect with your heart.

Now, without looking to your past or to your memories, ask yourself: Who am I?

Experience this practice through your feelings and simply allow yourself to feel, for as much time as you consider necessary.

Finally, at the end of the practice, express your hope that this meditation will be of benefit to all beings without exception.

Experiment:

Five monkeys were put in a room. In the center of the room there was a ladder and at the top of it were some bananas. Whenever one of the monkeys climbed the ladder to get the bananas, the scientists sprayed cold water on the rest of them. After a while, the monkeys made the connection between using the ladder and getting sprayed with cold water, so whenever one of then ventured onto the ladder to get a banana, the other monkeys violently prevented him from doing so. In the end, despite the temptation of eating something delicious, no monkey dared to climb the ladder.

At that point, the scientists removed one of the initial monkeys and put a new one in the room.

The new monkey naturally climbed up the ladder to get the bananas at the top of it. When the others saw what he was trying to do, they threw themselves on him and forced him down before the spray of cold water came. After several attempts, the new monkey understood that it was better for his physical integrity to give up all thoughts of climbing the ladder.

The scientists again replaced one of the monkeys from the initial group. When this new monkey tried to climb the ladder, the monkey that had arrived before him participated in the attacks with particular zeal.

The same process was then repeated with the third, fourth and fifth monkey, until the time came when all of the monkeys in the initial experiment had been replaced.

At that point, the scientists discovered something surprising: although none of the monkeys in the room had ever been sprayed with cold water, none of them dared climb the ladder to get the bananas. If the primates could have been asked why they did not climb the ladder to get the food, the answer would probably have been: "I don't know. It's always been this way".

Chapter 31: The day I let go of everything and allowed life simply to be

"It doesn't matter how many sacred words you have read, or how many you have said; they are worth nothing if you do not act in accordance with them".

Buddha

"When you let go, you fly".

Mr. Díaz

For many years I thought the only way to live was the way my family and my environment had taught me (or, on occasions, imposed on me): getting a good job that would provide for me in the future... What did it matter whether or not I liked or felt realized doing that job? As a result I felt tremendous pressure to live a "normal" life, out of loyalty to the ideology professed by my family, friends and all those defenders in general of this paradigm of normality which, deep in my heart, I felt was absolutely insane and also meaningless.

My determination to search outside for what was already inside led me to begin various relationships that ended up causing an even greater sense of disconnection and distress, and at the same time I felt a heavy feeling of resignation, due to the total dichotomy I was experiencing between my desire for freedom and the continuous struggle to earn a living and garner the appreciation of others. I would have to go through various necessary and revealing situations to be able to discover what it really means to live.

As the days went by, I slowly discovered and began to apply all the teachings and tools from the masters that I found along the way. The process of reencountering my true nature was now unstoppable.

I went through a series of jobs. The last one led me to an experience that contributed a great deal to the awakening that would radically change my life. I worked for an airline and after a long flight the entire crew had two days off to rest in Singapore. There, to pass the time, we went inside an art gallery. I had always felt that painting was what really spoke to my heart but at that point it had been a long time since I last picked up a brush. Seeing the beautiful paintings in the gallery had an enormous impact on me: their blues reminded me of my early works in which I tried to convey the essence of the ocean. Tears welled up in my eyes and began to flow. That crying was like nothing I had ever felt before; it was crying that came from the deepest part of my soul. Afterwards I felt I was in a state of rapture and the sensation lasted all day long. A great force that was rising inside me whispered to me from my heart: "Stop struggling against life and let go... Share... Let yourself live without resisting".

And, after that experience, that is exactly what I did. I felt full of joy, overflowing with happiness for no apparent reason. One week later I had the experience with Sami, the young man from Bangladesh, whom I wrote about in Chapter 4. That experience further contributed to my awakening and gave me the push I needed to decide to let go of everything: I offered my life to the Universe so that, from that moment on, it could do as it wished with me. Here's something interesting: a Tibetan lama and good friend of mine divided the word Universe into "*uni*" (unity, one) and "*verse*" (poem). In other words, a "single verse," that of Love.

So I went back home determined to share and to create, with a Tibetan bowl and a Tibetan bell as my entire arsenal.

It did not take long for me to feel a sense of liberation and peace that was truly indescribable (a state of total presence and connection with everything), although it did not take very long for the opposition of my family, friends and others to appear, people who, innocently, because they knew no other paradigm than the one they had learned, completely disapproved of my decision. They were afraid of it. They considered it madness, and some believed it was even dangerous. Many of the details appear in the following chapters... In any case, I can say that my family's rejection was such that for years there was a great distance between us and a tremendous lack of communication, to the extent that my mother once called me, in tears, and asked with great anguish:

—Why couldn't I have had a normal son?

I viewed this situation with total acceptance, understanding and respect, while walking in connection with the call that Life had made for me to fulfill my purpose following the dictates of my heart.

Today my relationship with my family is thoroughly harmonious: they accept, understand and support me, with affection, on my path.

Since I made that decision, I give courses in which I share different "tools for the awakening of consciousness" that my fabulous teachers have taught me. I give classes on meditation and on releasing fears, workshops on Reiki and Tibetan energy therapies... In some of these workshops we have even walked on burning embers, saying goodbye to our limiting beliefs and proving to ourselves that we can move from the impossible to the possible. Many of these individual and group sessions are the source of the true stories I tell in this book.

I also organize "gong baths," which are concerts of harmonizing music with different instruments (Tibetan bowls, quartz bowls and handpans combined with clarinet, violin, piano, sitar...); in them, the members of the audience not only enjoy the music but simultaneously are filled with peace and healing vibrations.

Once in a while I also organize exhibitions of my paintings. The works I show are paintings created from the heart, with the desire that everyone near them can become free of the causes of suffering.

At this very instant I am fully present, enjoying the writing of this book, sipping a cup of tea and with no expectation other than the hope that it will be useful to others in reconnecting with their true essence.

With deep gratitude and appreciation, and thanks to all the wonderful beings with whom I come into contact every day, I keep remembering the path by which we can return to the self and deepen our understanding of the true nature of the mind.

Thanks to that decision to let go of everything, I now live fully and my life is one of total acceptance and neutrality. I have stopped looking for happiness and instead have become it, allowing things to simply be, feeling joy, creating, sharing, and letting life be what it truly is.

(In silence, allow yourself to simply feel)

Story:

In a remote village in India there lived a wise man who was much esteemed for his good advice, for his remarkable willingness to help others and for the love and calm he radiated at all times.

People appreciated him so much that he was always surrounded by many of the village's inhabitants. However, this popularity planted the seed of envy in three of his neighbors, who decided to do something to unmask the man who, they thought, was nothing but a quack.

So, on the wise man's birthday, they took a vase and filled it with garbage they had gathered specifically for the occasion, which included the excrements of various animals, rotten fish, dead insects... They wrapped it up like a gift and went to the master's house.

There was a long line of people who had come from near and far to honor the wise man on his birthday. He accepted each of their gifts and very graciously unwrapped them one by one, showing them to all those present.

When their turn came, these three individuals went up and, with gestures of scorn, gave him the package. Everyone was speechless when they saw what was inside the wrapping. Everyone except the wise man, who, without saying a word and smiling all the while, walked to the house: he carefully washed the vase, he filled it with the purest water available and he put his garden's most beautiful flower in it. And with the calm and love that characterized him, he returned the vase to his neighbors with the following words:

—You have friends here. This is my gift to you. Because one can give only what one has inside.

Chapter 32: Theft and attacks

"All humanity is one undivided and indivisible family.
I cannot detach myself from the wickedest soul".

Mahatma Gandhi

"You and me, we are one. I cannot hurt you without hurting myself".

Mahatma Gandhi

Sometimes unexpected things happen. It is at such times that we must learn to manage our emotions and be able to see difficult situations as an opportunity for inner discovery.

For a certain period of time I had to go live abroad for professional reasons, so I needed to find a place to leave my paintings while I was away. A friend of mine offered to keep them for me at her sister's house: they had an extra room and assured me that it would be no trouble at all...

The paintings would be safe, so I could rest easy and I could get them back any time. I could even go check on them if I came home on vacation. I must say that they were very nice to me so I decided to accept the offer and I left a collection of about 50 paintings with them. Since the family liked art, I told them they could hang some of them around the house, which they did.

Everything was just fine until, two years later, I came back to the island to live and I called this family to arrange to get my paintings back. I was truly grateful for the favor they had done me and I had decided to give them a couple of paintings for them to keep. However, these people showed resistance and were no longer nice.

They went so far as to demand that I give them four paintings of their choice in exchange for the "favor" that they had done for me. A major surprise came when, after picking up the paintings a week or two later, I took them to my new apartment: seven were missing (among them were the ones that they had demanded as payment, which were to be the main pieces of an exhibition I had a few months later). Over and over again I carefully checked the inventory list I had prepared two years earlier, the day I took the works to this family's house. I was sure of it; those seven canvases had "disappeared," they had vanished into thin air.

I wanted to think it had been a mistake, so I contacted them to inform them of the situation. Their reaction was hostile. Even though I told them several times that I was not accusing them of anything, they adopted a victim attitude that was quite surreal: "With everything we have done for you! This is how you pay us back? By calling us thieves?" I repeated that I was making no accusations, I just wanted to know if perhaps the paintings had been misplaced or left behind in some forgotten room.

They tried to play the guilt game to make me feel bad by any means possible, first playing the role of the poor victim slandered by my shameless accusations, then threatening to sue me (even today I don't know on what grounds). I couldn't understand it. I felt like I was in the middle of an argument between deaf people, in which no matter how loud you shouted nobody listened and whatever you said was misunderstood. The paintings had been there, I had taken them to their house two years ago. It said so clearly on the list and the family had even demanded them as payment just a few weeks earlier!

I found myself caught up in a completely inexplicable and toxic story consisting of attacks and insults. "But you spiritual people aren't supposed to get angry," they actually said. All of this made me very uncomfortable and confused. So I chose peace: I absolutely and totally accepted the situation; I decided to let it go, to forgive it all (to hand my awareness over to love and understanding) and to affectionately walk away from these people.

I told myself that it was a great opportunity to grow, to let go, to acknowledge the mirrors that life put before me... and to paint even better paintings! So I simply said thank you to life, I filled myself with compassion for this family and myself and moved on, letting go of any possible resentment and sending them love. Afterward, I felt totally liberated and in absolute peace.

What do the masters say?

In a dual world, where many people live as victims of reactionary thinking and its poisons, you sometimes find yourself in situations that seem to be attacks for no reason. At times like these, if your priority is truly peace, you will be calm and there will be no room for conflict. You will take the opportunity to free yourself, since life puts mirrors in front of us so that we can really cleanse ourselves of any disconnection with love. Understand that people do nothing to you; it is your ego that thinks they are doing it and it takes it personally. Life does not put you in any situation that you cannot overcome.

The only thing that feels attacked and has the need to defend itself is the ego, since our true nature is love and absolute acceptance.

People are not "bad," they just act in ignorance, victims of this potent poison created by the mind and its programs. If you act in the same frequency, you will be immersed in the conflict, because every time you attack you will be attacking yourself. This does not mean, however, that — if you are physically attacked and your life is in danger — you do not defend yourself.

Ask yourself: Which do I prefer? To be right or to be happy? This question will help you gain perspective and can even help you avoid illness.

In the words of these teachers: when you attack someone, either physically or mentally, you are in fact attacking yourself, God and life itself.

What do the masters do?

They feel compassion for all beings without exception.

They understand that the attack is only in the conflict-oriented mental program, and not in your essence or your true self.

They understand that people who react with hostility are, in truth, ignorant (their actions are caused by that mental poison).

They understand that people "do things" but do not "do things to you".

They give thanks when they find people that serve as a mirror. They make a priority of choosing peace.

They use tools to correct their awareness.

They look at the situation through the eyes of their true self or their essence (which is pure Love) with a gaze that accepts everything.

They hand their awareness over to Love.

What do the masters not do?

They do not judge.

They do not condemn.

They do not take things personally (they know that this is the favorite trap of the ego and its victim-oriented programs).

They do not feel offended. They do not insult others.

They do not fight someone else's attitude or any type of situation.

They do not feel attacked.

They take every opportunity to liberate themselves.

Practice:

In Hawaii there were ancient tribes that used an effective system to correct erroneous perception. They called it Ho'oponopono, which etymologically means "to correct a mistake". This tool is being spread to other parts of the world thanks to the marvelous work of Dr. Len.

The idea is basically that we take responsibility in the conflicts in which we have somehow become involved. Everything we perceive is a projection of our mind; that is, we have created it ourselves. Therefore, when we use *Ho'oponopono*, we are cleansing the erroneous perception that has been projected from a place without love or from a place of judgment. To practice *Ho'oponopono*, we think of that person or situation we want to heal and we say:

I am sorry, because up until now I was not aware of my responsibility.

Forgive me for not having seen you with eyes of love, as part of myself and as a perfect and innocent being.

Thank you for giving me the opportunity to cleanse my erroneous perception and my judging gaze.

I love you.

That is where healing and a change in perception occur.

With the simple and powerful words: *I'm sorry, Forgive me, Thank you, I love you*; the conscious mind can begin the process of *Ho'oponopono* and thus free itself of its memories. The alternative is to stay enslaved to them, plagued with guilt and resentment. You decide!

Find a quiet place and connect with your heart or with your essence. From that place, think of a situation or of some being toward which you feel a certain resistance or anger, and say the following words, feeling the meaning of each of them: *"I'm sorry, Forgive me, Thank you, I love you"*.

This practice can also be carried out during your daily activities, whenever a situation of tension or distress arises. Simply say these words to yourself (you don't have to say them aloud to the person in front of you, because this is an internal practice) and notice what happens in your mind, the beautiful change in perception that takes place inside you.

Think how marvelous it would be if you could view all events in a neutral way.

Story:

A little boy was waiting for his father to get home from work. When he saw his father come through the door, he asked him quietly, with eyes full of admiration:

—Papa, how much do you earn per hour?

The father glared at the boy and replied:

—Son, what kind of a question is that? Come on, don't bother me now. I'm tired. —Papa, just tell me please how much you earn per hour.

The father decided to answer him and, with a voice full of resignation, he said. —10 Euros an hour.

—¿Papa, could you lend me 5 Euros?

The father became angry and said harshly:

—So that's why you wanted to know how much I earn! Go to bed and don't bother me, you selfish boy!

Later that evening the father, after reflecting on what had happened, felt guilty. He told himself that perhaps his son needed the money for something he wanted to buy... To ease his conscience he went to the boy's room and asked him:

—Are you asleep, son?

—No —said the boy sleepily.

—Well, here's the money you asked me for —said the father, showing a bill to the child.

—Thanks, Dad! —exclaimed the child.

Then he put his hand under the pillow and pulled out a handful of coins.

—Now I have 10 Euros. Could I buy an hour of your time?

Chapter 33: Children and hyperactivity

"We cannot change anything unless we first accept it.
Condemnation does not liberate, it oppresses".

Carl G. Jung

Adela was desperate. She didn't know what to do with her six-year-old daughter, who had been diagnosed with hyperactivity. At home, she said, her daughter drove her insane, and at school the girl could not focus on anything. In fact, she was now being given medication. Adela even said that having a daughter like that was torture and if she had known it would be like this, she never would have had children.

Based on my experience in treating similar cases, I told her that a hyperactive child is only asking for love and attention, like the very words used to refer to this condition suggest "ATTENTION deficit and hyperactivity disorder". Just look at the statistics: currently, hyperactivity is almost a plague, while in our generation (both of us were born in 1970) it was not so common. Perhaps this is because, since people lived less stressful lives, they were able to pay more attention and show more affection to children... And, especially, because back then our relationships with others were more intimate and less superficial. I told her that one of my teachers always said that the word intimate meant to be present and be one with another.

I asked her what her reaction was when the little girl was acting restlessly. She told me that she shouted, she sent her to her room or she put her in front of the TV. I suggested that instead of that reactionary response she should try putting her hand on her hair and, sweetly and patiently, look in her eyes and ask her sincerely how she felt. It seemed to me that it would be good if the mother took the time to listen to and share in the feelings of her daughter.

I still remember how she stared at me and asked:

—And that's it? Just that? I've tried everything: pills, psychologists, special educators, counselors, but nothing changes.

—Yes. But what you probably haven't tried is that loving way of giving attention and affection.

Adela left my office determined to try the new tool that very afternoon. One week later I received a call from her: the little girl had shown great improvement. Not only was she much more relaxed but all symptoms of hyperactivity had disappeared. The girl had even begun to show interest in the activities that her mother did every morning, yoga and meditation.

Some time later, Adela told me a sweet story: both of them were doing a Tibetan yoga posture that Adela had learned at one of my "Yoga of Happiness" workshops. The posture was slightly uncomfortable, so the girl asked her mother why they did this weird, but fun, stuff...

—To obtain mental calm, my dear —responded Adela. A few seconds later, the girl had another question: —And how long will it take for this mental calm to get here?

Today, three years after that initial consultation, the girl is doing wonderfully; she is happy and calm, and displays not a single sign of hyperactivity. Of course, she was never medicated again.

What do the masters say?

Your child is a part of you, a continuation of you that will form future generations. It is a reflection of you. Treat it with dedication and affection.

Start with yourself: if you dedicate time and affection to yourself it will be easier for you to do the same with your child.

What do the masters do?

They listen to and spend time with children and at the same time they learn from them.

They show sincere interest in how they are doing and they act patiently with them.

They treat them like true masters of life. They give them freedom to express themselves.

They show them that they are important and loved. They learn from them.

They play with them.

What do the masters not do?

They do not look the other way or act as if the children were a nuisance.

They do not think that medication is the answer.

They do not hit them or insult them.

They do not think that children will raise themselves. Rather, they raise them with freedom and affection.

They do not lose their patience.

They do not miss the opportunity to learn from them.

They do not try to change them.

They do not impose ideas or concepts.

Practice:

Give your child full attention and be present for him or her. As you gently touch the child's head or rub his or her shoulder, ask sincerely how the child feels, what state she is in. Listen to your child without interrupting. Do it with love.

This same practice you can do with yourself as well, in front of the mirror.

Afterwards, hope that this practice brings benefits to all beings without exception.

Story:

A man goes to the psychologist and says: —Doctor, I have a problem.

The psychologist shows the man a sheet of paper with ink stains and asks:

—What do you see?

The man says:

—An elephant copulating with a giraffe.

The psychologist shows him another sheet of paper and asks: —What do you see?

—A man spying on an elephant —he answers. The psychologist shows him a third sheet and asks again:

—What do you see?

—A man and an elephant under a bed —he responds without hesitation. The psychologist thinks for a minute and says:

—Sir, I believe you are preoccupied by elephants.

—You fool! —replies the man —It's not my fault! You're the one who keeps showing me pictures of elephants!

Chapter 34:
Limiting beliefs or programs

"If you want to learn about your past, then look at your present, which is the result: if you want to learn about your future, look at your present, which is the cause".

Buddha

"One does not become enlightened by imagining figures of light, but by making the darkness conscious... What does not become conscious manifests in our lives as fate".

Carl G. Jung

Elena is a young woman I met several years ago. Up until that time, all of her relationships had, in her words, been total disasters, because all her boyfriends ended up breaking up with her suddenly. So she had reached the conclusion that all men are the same: toxic beings who did not appreciate her and who treated her badly, causing her to suffer.

She had recently started a new relationship, though, with a young man who seemed different from the rest. He was attentive, understanding, affectionate... Everything she had always dreamed of. However, she was not entirely sure about the situation. Most likely it would turn out badly and he would leave her, just like the others had. Yes, it would most likely be yet another failure. And naturally, with thoughts like these, that is exactly what happened: two months later, the boyfriend broke up with her, leaving her disconsolate and convinced that her theory was right. It's because all men are the same, right?

I took the opportunity to talk to her about the "self-fulfilling prophesy": this is when you take a certain experience and create a belief that you think is true, and life, like the mirror it is, gives you more of that kind of experience, which serves to reinforce your system of beliefs and thus locks you into a vicious circle that you yourself have created. Your prediction of the future ends up becoming the cause that makes it come true. When an athlete runs to break an Olympic record, he does not think "I'm not going to make it, I'll probably trip and fall, goodbye to all my dreams"... No. He concentrates on his goal and he does everything in his power to reach it.

There is a fabulous illustration of this that I learned from Mr. Díaz and that shows perfectly how our limiting beliefs mark the tempo of our lives. Imagine that there is an orchestra conductor inside our subconscious, a man who, no matter what happens, constantly tells us that the worst possibility will come true and that if something can turn out badly, then it no doubt will. We give sheet music to the musicians: fantastic compositions, works of unequalled beauty; but the orchestra director modifies them and gives them his own "musical" criteria, so it doesn't matter how lovely the melody is, the musicians always end up playing a funeral march.

So, just as this fictitious director is an expert in transforming waltzes into requiems with his baton, we do the same when we turn the opportunities for expansion and happiness that appear in our life into genuine nightmares... and all because of our limiting or dysfunctional beliefs.

So, our task is to urgently change these toxic beliefs that are creating the soundtrack of our life. It must be us, and not these beliefs, that decide which symphony we like best. Thus, if there is an area or field in your life in which things are not quite the way you would like them to be, you should try looking at your beliefs: there is probably at least one belief that is separating you from what you really are, from your dreams or from Life with a capital L.

Another illustrative image is the following. Imagine that during our childhood, at the age of 6 or 7, we put on underwear that will never wear out and can never be taken off. Imagine the pain and discomfort it would cause us as we grow up: think of the distress we would experience during our teens, our twenties, thirties, forties, sixties, eighties... It would undoubtedly affect our flow, our promenade through life. But we would become accustomed to living this way, uncomfortable, in pain... To say nothing of the smell!

The same occurs with our beliefs. If we notice that they are getting too small for us, that they no longer fit, or even that they start to smell bad... change them for others that are larger! Or, even better, let go of them all! According to my teachers, life begins where our beliefs end.

Elena understood that her relationships were but a reflection of how she herself felt at the time. If she undervalued herself and felt small, that is what she would find outside, in this case with partners who ended up being a mirror, doing the same to her that she did to herself. I suggested that she stop treating herself that way, that she stop looking outside to compensate for her inner needs. After a six-month period during which Elena consciously spent time alone and dedicated time and love to herself, she met a new man with whom she continues to enjoy good times and happiness.

To complement this story, I would like to share the following anecdote:

In one of my first encounters with the Tibetan monk and master Kalu T., I asked him about levitation.

—In the Himalayas we have seen some lamas that levitate —he told me with his funny childlike smile and with a gleam in his eyes.

—Really?

—Yes, really! I have seen it with my own eyes! —And how do they do it? —I asked him. —Because nobody ever told them that it can't be done.

—I see... So, Kalu, can you also levitate? —No, not me. I was told that it was impossible.

Dear reader, have you ever wondered how many narrow and limiting beliefs are oppressing your free flow through this adventure called life?

What do the masters say?

Toxic and limiting beliefs are truly harmful and noxious for human beings, since our body, mind and spirit need to be nourished by love, which is what we really are. In contrast, those poisons feed on fear and attack. Thus, to live under their influence disconnects us gradually from the love that comprises our essence and ensures our well-being; and we suffer the consequences at various levels (physical, mental, emotional...). Truly, to fall under the influence of these thoughts disconnected from love is like voluntarily ingesting poison. There is a great phrase that illustrates this perfectly: "To hate someone is as absurd as taking poison and hoping that the other person will die". All the teachers I have known emphasize the importance of being alert against these poisons, so as to be able to live in harmony.

Nowadays we can find numerous scientific studies that demonstrate the direct relationship between the emotions we feel and our immune system: a certain emotion felt continually over a period of time causes a mental state that has a biological impact on our bodies, for example, on our defenses. This is what the medical doctor and writer Bruce H. Lipton means when he says "if you change your thoughts, you change your biology".

There are many people who, under the influence and interference of this mental toxicity (ignorance), generate dysfunctional beliefs that lead to constant suffering. These are beliefs such as: "I'm worthless," "I'm not good enough," "life is hard," "we're here to suffer"... These persons, shaped by these beliefs and considering them proven by the suffering they produce, never live life fully. Instead they merely exist or get by however they can, thinking that happiness is a utopian ideal. It is clearly a vicious circle: dysfunctional beliefs cause suffering, and in turn this suffering reinforces and reaffirms such beliefs.

It is vital that we all take responsibility for escaping from this cycle and understand that in truth happiness is not a utopia: it is our natural state. Happiness is already inside us, but the walls and barriers that we have built use fear and its poisons as cement, and they separate us from that happiness.

Practice:

My teachers have conveyed to me that for one to be really happy one must appreciate, since, according to their teachings, appreciation is the fusion of love, acceptance and gratitude.

This simple but powerful practice consists of feeling, today and everyday, appreciation.

Begin every phrase with: *"I love the feeling that..."*

This exercise will help you attain a mental state of peace and joy.

Every time you finish, express your hope that this practice will bring benefits to all beings without exception.

Story:

—What is love?

—It is the total absence of fear —said the teacher.

—And what is it that we fear?

—Love —responded the teacher.

Anthony de Mello

Chapter 35: Fear and superstitions

"He who fears suffering is already suffering from fear".

Chinese proverb

"Fear is only truly lethal when you give it your power and make it your guide".

Mr. Díaz

I remember Mr. Díaz telling me a real story about a friend of his who was very worried about his future. This friend, Marco, was so preoccupied that he decided to visit a well-known clairvoyant to ask him what the tarot cards said about his fate. Among other things, the cards revealed that within a short period of time (sometime during that year), Marco would die in a serious accident involving a great deal of rubble.

Given the seriousness of the matter and the trust he had in the clairvoyant, Marco decided to take all possible precautions. To avoid the dreaded accident, he radically changed his lifestyle. The first step was to stop using his car, the next was to stop going out for the leisurely strolls he enjoyed so much. In the end he simply stayed at home as much as he could. He was falling straight into obsession: he was so fearful and anxious about what he believed was an imminent danger that he even had to take a medical leave from work. He spent all day in fear, thinking that something bad would happen, seeing danger all around him. He even stopped going out to do the shopping: he ordered everything by Internet to avoid any situation of risk. He lived with the expectation that something terrible would happen.

One day, at around one in the afternoon, a time of day in which Marco normally would have been working (his work day was from 8 to 4) there was a big explosion in the building: one of the neighbors had accidentally left the gas canister open. All morning long it leaked gas, which combusted when somebody lit a cigarette. When the canister exploded, the roof of the building collapsed and Marco died instantly under an avalanche of rubble.

Yet another example of how our fears and pessimistic expectations end up attracting whatever it is that we fear.

What do the masters say?

Fear is the absence of love and a lack of trust in life. Choosing to live in the absence of life will always, sooner or later, manifest in your experience. Your beliefs and expectations create realities; they mark and shape your existence. If you live under a cloud of superstition and negativity, your thoughts become the forecast of your future. In other words, what you fear will come true.

We create what we think: so, if we have our mind on illness and death, that is doubtless what we will draw to us. It is essential that we become aware of such negative thoughts, and correct them or disassociate ourselves from them, given their very powerful energy, which can end up creating the very things you fear.

The mechanism I have just described also works in the opposite direction: if you think about and focus on what you love, that is what you will experience in your life.

The first step that must be taken to change our painful experiences is to modify the nature of our thoughts and, along with them, of our perception, which so heavily conditions the quality of our lives. Once you have reached that point, it will become easier not to identify so closely with your thoughts.

Fear is suffering prefabricated by your mind and therefore, if you change your perception and choose to see the world with eyes of love, acceptance and gratitude, your life will be transformed into joy and peace.

The masters tell us that nothing that can happen to us is as terrible as the damage caused by living in a state of fear.

The master J. Kim has come up with an excellent definition of fear. He says it is "a kind of insurance company that gives us a false feeling of security and comfort in the short term, in exchange for mortgaging our life, freedom and dreams". At the beginning we are very satisfied with the service and benefits and with the premium we pay; however, over time we begin to feel that the price was too high: it has cost us, literally, our life.

What do the masters do?

They see things in perspective and correct any erroneous vision (mental filters that result in non-life or in distrust of life).

They focus on what they love, on solutions, on life, because this is always their top priority. For them, it is easy, because they love without exception.

They live in gratitude, as if each day were the last, with intensity and trust.

They use phrases such as "I hope that when death comes for me, it finds me full of life," because they understand that life is in the here and now, and that to live with *preoccupation* is to be concerned with illusory projections about the future.

They talk about what they love. They walk hand-in-hand with life.

They perceive the world choosing love as their teacher.

They know that death will come, sooner or later; for this reason they prefer to live intensely, without attachments or fears, in freedom.

They always choose love, which gives life, instead of fear, which leads to *non-life*.

When facing a complicated situation they ask themselves: "right now, what am I choosing? Life or *non-life*? Trust or fear?"

And they act in consequence, always choosing to live, so as not to feel like the living dead.

What do the masters not do?

They do not live in fear, nor do they give energy to that which they fear.

They do not generate thoughts or expectations about accidents or death.

They do not allow themselves to be seized by distorted visions, such as negative prophecies: they know that these visions are a figment of the ego that is living in conflict and fear.

They do not swap their health for a false sense of security.

They do not isolate themselves to avoid suffering because they know that doing so is useless and unnecessary suffering in itself. They know that if you do such a thing, you are already defeated.

Practice:

If you are afraid of death, or if you have some superstition or "negative prophecy" floating around your head, try the following practice.

Seated in your favorite meditation position, take at least three deep breaths while you observe and accept how you feel. Make the following affirmations:

"I am letting go of everything false that disconnects me from life. Those projections come from fear, they are not me and they are not real".

Focus your attention on your heart, on the spot between the two halves of your ribcage, and be aware of this spot for at least a few minutes.

Then, inhale and make the following affirmation:

"I am taking back my inner power, my life and my trust".

And as you exhale, say:

"I am releasing all that is false, everything that is non-life".

Finally, say thank you for this new day. And express your hope that this meditation will benefit all beings without exception.

Story:

A Zen master was walking down the street when a man ran up and hit him as hard as he could. The master fell down. Then he got up and kept walking in the same direction as before, without even looking behind him. The disciple who was walking with the master was astounded and he exclaimed:

—Who was that man? What's going on here? If you act like that, anybody can just come up to you and kill you! And you didn't even look at the person! You don't know who it is or why he did that!

To all this the master said:

—That's his problem, not mine.

Chapter 36:
Intense compassion and freedom

"When an inner situation is not made conscious,
it will appear outside as fate".

Carl G. Jung

"Want to stop belonging to the number of slaves?
Break your chains and rid yourself of all fear and spite".

Epictetus

From time to time we come across people who have settled into attitudes of disconnection with life, victims of a conflict-oriented mindset, who —out of ignorance— make great efforts to create fear in those around them. There are times in life in which one must stand up and speak assertively (although also with compassion and understanding) to these beings who display toxic behavior, especially when it is a member of the family. I would like to share an experience my family went through, something that happened that shows quite clearly the type of action I am talking about.

My father, as I have already mentioned, was a great teacher to me. Without him, I never would have discovered all that I am now experiencing. And I want to clarify that, despite what the following story might suggest, my love for my father is absolutely infinite, sincere and unconditional.

One day at lunchtime, my sister, who that day was feeling kind of emotional, asked our father why, in all her thirty years of life, he had never hugged her or told her that he loved her. My father responded the only way he knew how, launching an attack: he started criticizing her, highlighting the flaws that, in his opinion, she had and the things he thought she had done wrong over the years. I witnessed the scene as a mere observer, until I decided to participate, moved by love:

—Listen to the question again, Dad. Your daughter is just asking for a little affection. When he heard that, all my father's anger focused on me and, for a few minutes, I had to listen to a series of reproaches in which my father recriminated me for all the ways that, in his mind, I had failed him as a son: not having a "normal career" and doing "strange stuff"... During those minutes I looked at him with total acceptance, and despite all the rejection that he was sending my way with each one of his words, I felt only love. I saw how determined he was to continue with his mental programs and his attack-oriented patterns, so I decided, moved by that love I felt, to speak assertively to him, acting at all times out of compassion and understanding.

—Ok, Dad. Since for you it is so hard to say anything positive about your children, I am going to say something positive about you. Every time someone asks him who my greatest teacher was, a Japanese or Tibetan monk, perhaps, or a meditation teacher, a lama... I always say no. None of them has taught me as much as you have. I tell them that there is no doubt that my father has been and still is my best teacher, the person to whom I owe the biggest lessons in my life.

When he heard this, his eyes opened as wide as plates. I went on:

—And for me you are a great teacher because you have shown me something very important, very powerful: The example of a conditioned life. If I had followed in your footsteps, taking those actions that you wanted to impose on me, on more than one occasion, now I would be a person trapped by appearances, a person who lives only in the past, a person who sees and focuses on only the negative aspects of others. I would have problems with my friends and my family. I would show no affection ever, not even to my own children. And I would never change, because I would think that I am always right and everyone else is wrong.

At that moment, my father dropped the glass of wine he was holding. Then he pounded his fist on the table and, with a face full of fury, stood up and stomped through the door.

My sister was crying and my mother was staring at me in amazement, realizing that I had just shown my father a mirror so that he could see his own image.

Right then an enormous release and expansion took place, not just in me but in the rest of the family as well. The truly interesting thing was that after a few minutes, my father came back and gave each of us a hug for the first time in our lives: first my sister and then me. After that day, my relationship with my father healed and entered a state of complete harmony, because my words had come from love.

What do the masters say?

In Buddhism, the aim of intense compassion is to free yourself and other beings from all types of deception and illusion; it enables us to live in unity and innocence and it eliminates any type of obstacle to awakening, so that we can cease to live in ignorance and stop causing suffering around us.

Although the name includes the word "intense" this type of compassion is used only when you have already completely forgiven and understood the situation or the person. The intention is never to hurt or impose your points of view or opinion, but rather to grow together and free yourselves of ego-oriented programs.

The great master Khempo (already mentioned in Chapter 9) would often say something along the lines of: "Make the firm decision to be happy instead of being right. When you let go of the need to control and change others and decide to focus on your own life (the here and now), you are giving yourself the best gift possible: peace, freedom and real happiness".

What do the masters do?

They understand that they are not their family, they simply have arrived in the world through that family; therefore, they do not allow their freedom or their path to be conditioned by their family.

Moved by love and respect, they give people tips on how to stop suffering, although they know that these people, abducted by their conflict-oriented programs, will feel they are being attacked.

They share their tools (without imposing them) when they see they have the opportunity and see that they are necessary.

They are aware that love cannot be imposed, only proposed. They know that sometimes the best way to help is not to help.

Sometimes they put a mirror up to a person who has been abducted by his or her conflict-oriented mindset.

They free themselves and others. This simple act prevents illnesses in them and others (cancer, multiple sclerosis, fibromyalgia, etc).

What do the masters not do?

They are not hypocritical.

They are not condescending.

They do not act as accomplices to people who are destroying themselves and their surroundings.

They do not live to please others, even if those others are members of the family.

They do not take part in the lies or the games of the ego's conflict-oriented mental program.

They do not stay in toxic emotional places at the expense of their physical, mental or emotional well-being.

They do not impose.

They do not resign themselves to situations they dislike.

They do not resist.

They do not renounce their inner peace.

Practice:

Be compassionately sincere with yourself and with your surroundings, choosing to use words that come from love, not fear.

You will feel truly free and peaceful.

Every time you do this, express your hope that this act of liberation will bring benefits to all beings without exception.

Story:

One day the teacher asked:

—Why do people shout when they are angry? The monks thought about this.

—Because we lose control —said one of them. That's why we shout.

—But why shout when the other person is right next to you? Nobody said anything, so the teacher finally said:

—When two people are angry, their hearts move apart from each other. To cover that distance they must shout, in order to hear one another. The angrier they are, the further apart their hearts will be and the louder they will have to shout to be able to hear each other.

Then the master asked:

—What happens when two people fall in love?

—They talk quietly to each other, because their hearts are very close together. The distance between them is very small.

Whenever you argue, do not let your hearts move away from each other, do not say words that will distance them even further, because the day may come when the distance is so great that they cannot find the way back to each other.

Meher Baba

Chapter 37: Friends who reject us

"Birds born in a cage think flying is an illness".

Alejandro Jodorowsky

"Friendship can only happen through the development
of mutual respect and in a spirit of sincerity".

Dalai Lama

Luis was one of my best friends. We went to the same grade school and, since we were little, we had had many great moments and countless adventures together. He was one of those great childhood friends that you always remember fondly, one of those friends you know you can count on no matter what and whom you are willing to help however you can in any situation or circumstances.

When I decided to let go of everything and give in to my function in this life, I perceived that, as I got closer to that path of freedom, Luis pulled further and further away, to the point that he stopped calling me. What started as a simple "cooling" of the relationship ended up turning into something much more distant: first he stopped calling me, and then he stopped answering the phone when I called him. Although I never listen to malicious comments made by other people, I will say that more and more people came up to me to tell me that Luis was saying bad things about me behind my back. One evening we saw each other by chance at a party and his behavior towards me was extremely cold, as if I had done something terrible to him, something I could not quite understand or remember. He even refused to acknowledge me when we crossed paths in the street. I did not give great importance to this and instead I let life follow its natural course. Since I had a clean conscience, I decided to let everything flow and not to interfere.

The years went by and I saw that my friend Luis lost almost all of his hair and gained a lot of weight. Plus, the image he conveyed was one of a sad person who was absent and deeply dissatisfied. One morning we bumped into each other at a café and, to my amazement, he came up to say hello and asked if he could sit down next to me. The conversation we had surprised me:

—José, I have to confess something to you. All this time I have been cold and distant with you because I hated you.

—You hated me? Isn't that kind of a strong word? —I inquired, surprised but smiling.

—Yes, it is. But every time I saw you or somebody mentioned you I remembered all those dreams that I kept postponing, making me live a life that I don't really want, living in a place I don't want to be, married to a person I no longer love, working at a job that I hate just so I can make the mortgage payment every month, and with no time whatsoever for me or for my dreams. So every time I saw you, you represented that part of me that I was allowing to die. And so I want to apologize for that... and also to ask for help.

—Luis, my friend, there is no need to apologize, because I am not in the least bit offended. You fell into one of the mental traps into which many of us fall. I will give you all the help I can and remember, I'll always love you like a brother no matter what —I answered.

We then gave each other a big heartfelt hug. We were talking all afternoon and I shared with him some tools to help him get out of the cage in which he had gotten stuck. One of the things he found most helpful was a simple question that has the power to get us out of the role of victim of the circumstances and to take us to a sense of responsibility and to our heart: Why am I doing this to myself?

Here we have a fine example of how quite often the criticism, the rejection and even the aggressiveness we receive from somebody for no apparent reason are in fact nothing but that person's defense mechanism. If we do not react, the conflict is not in us but rather in the other person's mindset. This means that instead of judging that person, the best response is probably feeling compassion and inspiration to help him or her (with a sense of responsibility).

Practice:

Think of a person with whom you have a conflict. Now repeat, feeling the power of these affirmations:

"I forgive myself for judging you".

"I free you of my judgment, I free myself of my judgment".

"You are innocent, I am innocent".

"I understand that all relationships are for discovering who I really am and for healing my mind".

"I understand that everyone acts according to his or her level of consciousness, which is often ignorance".

"I love you. I love myself".

Finally, express your hope that this meditation will bring benefits to all beings without exception.

Story:

The lover knocked at the door of his beloved.

—Who knocks? asked the beloved from within.

—It is I, said the lover.

—Go away. This house is not big enough for you and me.

The rejected lover went away into the desert. There he meditated for months on end, pondering the words of the beloved. Finally he returned and knocked at the door again.

—Who knocks?

—It is you.

And the door opened immediately.

Anthony de Mello

Chapter 38:
Weight gain and negative internal dialogue

"When we "put" the mind somewhere we are placing our attention: we are creating images in our mind or directing attention to a sense object. When we focus the mind on something, the object of focus affects the quality of consciousness and there are correlated changes in the body".

Tenzin Wangyal Rinpoche

"Tibetan Yogas of Dream and Sleep"
"Change the way you think and your body will respond accordingly".

Bruce Lipton

Dunia came to see me because she was very concerned about her weight. She had gained about 45 pounds in just over a month. Such a sudden increase was very strange, especially in such a young woman. I looked at her and asked at what point in her life she had begun saying mean things to herself.

It had all started two months earlier, following a break-up for which she felt she was to blame. From that time forward, she had been constantly telling herself "I'm stupid," "I'm worthless," "Nobody will ever love me," and "I'm always wrecking my relationships"...

I suggested, first of all, that she begin engaging in a positive dialogue with herself and that she come to terms with the event that had unleashed everything. I pointed out the possibility of understanding that things had happened just as they were supposed to, that things could not be any other way. Her actions had been the result of a certain state of consciousness; that is, she had done the best she could with the tools she had at the time. Now her task was to choose learning instead of pain. If she did, she would see results very quickly. Dunia claimed to understand me but said she could not find anything nice to say to herself. She did not even recognize herself in the mirror! She felt fat and ridiculous. As she looked at her reflection all she could see was ugliness in her face and body. So I encouraged her to look at the lovely blue eyes she had. And she did. She started by focusing on her beautiful eyes and, from there, she went on to see other parts of her body that she also liked. Every morning she looked at herself in the mirror and gave thanks for her health and other positive things about her, not just her body but her life. By doing so, she was gradually nourishing a positive internal dialogue. The result was spectacular: in a question of a month and a half, without following any special diet or going to the gym, Dunia lost those 45 pounds and returned to her normal weight. Simply by eliminating feelings of guilt, she recovered a healthy self-esteem: she let go of that negative burden that had made her retain liquids and gain weight.

Once again we can see the tremendous power that our words and our emotions have on our mind, our cells and our energy field.

What do the masters say?

They understand that it is very important to choose states of peace instead of states of war, especially if the war you are waging is against yourself. They understand that if you send messages of rejection and negativity to yourself, you are causing an impact on your body. Your inner being feeds on love, which is a very high vibrational frequency. When you move away from that frequency, your body reacts by letting you know that the choice you made was not a good one.

They understand that we do not make mistakes or fail, all we do is acquire the experiences necessary to keep growing throughout life.

Processes such as negative internal dialogue constitute a total disconnection with life; as a result, different signs begin to appear within us, manifestations of non-life, such as illness, pain, suffering... All of these responses are nothing but different manifestations of disharmony.

They understand that blaming yourself while looking back means losing your life in the present: guilt is a failure to update your perception. Your judgment of the past act takes place from a present moment in which you have knowledge and tools that you did not have when whatever it was happened. That is why it is so important to view what we consider "mistakes" with the right perspective, seeing them with the compassion we would feel for a child whose actions are guided by innocence and inexperience.

Mr. Díaz once told me about a person who went through a situation that filled him with guilt and resentment towards himself to such an extreme that in the period of one month he developed cancer and died. He produced so much emotional toxin that he actually disappeared in a very short period of time. As Mr. Díaz expressed it, in his always original way of speaking, "he guilted himself to death".

Kalu T. wisely describes this phenomenon: "If you see ugliness in the world, then the world will send it back to you; but if you see it in yourself, then your body and emotions will become that ugliness".

What do the masters do?

They always choose a conciliatory dialogue, a dialogue of peace, and they prefer inner silence.

They invigorate their soul based on a desire to improve, always from a place of joy and never from a place of guilt and resentment towards oneself.

They let go of burdens.

They let go of everything connected to fear.

They always look for that space of inner silence in which there is no self-judgment or self-criticism, that place where compassion and love reside.

They feel full acceptance.

They understand that everything happens for our awakening and our inner discovery.

What do the masters not do?

They do not blame themselves. They do not judge themselves.
They do not condemn themselves. They do not interpret.
They do not torture themselves.
They never choose conflict or war,
because that would disconnect them from life.
They do not make demands of themselves from a feeling of imposition
and resentment, but rather with a sense of joy, excellence and humor.
They do not use their memories as a guide.
They are not victims of their mistaken perception.

Practice:

Seated in a meditation position, breathe deeply and make these
affirmations as follows.
As you inhale: *"I feel love and oxygen flowing through each and every one of my cells".*
As you exhale: *"I feel tremendous love towards myself, my body and my life".*
As you inhale: *"I fill myself with joy and with life".*
As you exhale: *"I am letting go of any feeling of guilt or resentment. I choose peace".*
Afterwards, hope that this practice brings benefits to all beings without
exception.

A conscious letter:

Dear cancer,
Today I must bid you farewell, and I do so with the biggest of smiles.
Today I must say goodbye to you but I will certainly not forget you
because you have taught me a lesson in life. Today I must leave you

behind to start my new life, my life without you, which will be the same life, the only one I have, and the life I want to enjoy to the fullest, but also a different life, because thanks to you my perspective has changed.

Sorry for having felt scared when they said your name close to me, sorry for having felt terrified when they told me that you were inside me, sorry for having considered you my enemy at first, because later I learned that you were an ally and that the battle, if there ever was a battle, was against me, to help me overcome my fears; sorry for so many things and thank you, thank you, for so many other things.

They told me two things at the beginning of all this: one was not to be afraid of cancer, that cancer was an opportunity that life was giving me to bring out the best version of myself; the other thing was that when I accepted this process, when I felt that what I was living through was going to be good for me, you would disappear because you are simply a symbol, you appeared as a sign so that I would realize that something in me had to change. And I think that I have achieved it, and that is why I am now healthy. I would like to think that everything I have learned has contributed to recovering my health, in addition to the medical treatments.

So, today I bid you farewell. I have so much peace inside me that I will not even tell you not to come back; if you do appear again I will understand that despite my fears, you do it to help me because that is what life wants, because the Universe loves me.

Sincerely,
Ibán Bermúdez Betancor
(cancer patient who recovered in seven months; his full story, told in his own words, appears at the end of the book)

Reflection:

Be careful with your thoughts because your thoughts will become words.
Be careful with your words
because your words will become actions.

Be careful with your actions
because your actions will become habit.
Be careful with your habits because your habits will forge your values.
Be careful with your values
because your values will form your destiny.

Mahatma Gandhi

Chapter 39: Mindsets and mental programs that destroy us

"Every human being is the author of his own health or disease".

Buddha

*"For sure, one day the vulture of your mind will fly away;
people, now is the time to soar up to the heights".*

Padampa Sangye

*"Miracles are not contrary to nature; they are only contrary
to what we know about nature".*

Saint Augustine

This is something that happened not long ago. In fact, I was already busy working on this book. I remember that it was Tuesday. The doorbell rang. When I opened the door I found a middle-aged woman with a serious expression, pushing her husband's wheelchair. The husband, who was wearing an eye patch and had a shaved head, looked to be around 50.

The day before I had received a call from my friend Jezabel, who is a nurse. Through her work she had met this man, who was now examining my house and complaining bitterly of the smell of incense. The conversation in which Jeza asked me to see this man had been quite funny:

—He's a cancer patient. His case is quite...

—Ssshhh! I don't want to hear! —I cut her off before she could say any more. —I know, but the thing is, he has...

—That's enough! I don't want to know!

—Ok, ok, it's just that he has only...

—Stop! Don't take me the wrong way, but I would prefer that you not "contaminate" my mind with your medical prognosis —I cut her off once again, albeit in a friendly tone.

—I'd rather just see him, with no previous conditioning.

When we were seated in my office, I ask him to tell me why he had come. It did not take him long to answer: cancer in his left lung, and also a stroke he had had just one month ago and which had left him condemned to a wheelchair. He had tried everything but no allopathic treatment seemed to bring results. He had realized that it was his negative and reactionary mindset that had brought about this state, which caused so much suffering. So, he had decided to seek help... If someone could just show him how to change his mentality that made him, literally, self-destruct.

His wife told me a story that revealed the extent to which this negativity permeated our friend, who was always willing to share his cheerless attitude with anyone near enough to "enjoy" it. A few years earlier, at the funeral service held for his grandfather, who had also died of lung cancer, her husband had said aloud "One day I will get lung cancer, too". Staring at the floor all the while, the man confirmed the story:

—It's true. That's how I was...

The first thing I did was apologize in advance: what I was going to say might not be pleasant to hear at first. Following this little warning, I talked to him about the neutrality of the universe, which is vastly compassionate and impartial:

—So, of all the options you had that day at the funeral (winning the lottery, going on a vacation with your family, prosperity, health...) you go and decide to talk about lung cancer! And the universe, which as we just said is neutral and only gives you those experiences that you think you need, goes and gives you lung cancer, which is the experience you asked for. Well, there you go, enjoy it. Next time ask for a trip to Hawaii! —I commented with humor.

He started to see that he had always been angry with the world, that he tended to impose his vision on things, that he often felt undervalued and that, out of fear, he felt the need to control everything. To make matters worse, he now also felt guilty about being a burden to his family. He asked me to please help him.

I compared his story to that of a race horse: when he sets out toward the finish line, he gallops with all his might. No race horse ever stops running and stands still, feeling bad because people have bet on the wrong horse... In the same way, it was time for him to leave behind guilt and victimism and start running towards the goal like never before.

We looked at different tools (many of which are explained throughout this book) that would be useful to him in getting out of the reactionary mindset that is so good at making our bodies sick. After that we worked a little bit on his body's vibrations and his emotional and energy blockages.

When we were finished, I told him to stand up. At first he resisted. But then he managed to do it. I asked him to walk. He hesitated and, from the look he gave me, he must have thought I was insane... He had been in a wheelchair for a month! Nonetheless, he did it, to the amazement of his wife, who kept saying it was a miracle.

—A miracle —I explained to them—, is nothing but the reward you get for deactivating the limiting belief that tells you something is "impossible". In fact, our life goes far beyond our beliefs.

He could not believe it. He would take a few steps and then stop. Perplexed, all he could say was "but, but..." "No buts! Keep walking!" I told him. Deeply moved, he asked me if he would be able to walk from then on out. "Of course! And not just walk!" I took him out to the hallway and asked him to climb the stairs.

No words can describe how it felt for me to see them leave my house, the two of them pushing the wheelchair together, half laughing and half crying. Today Juan is doing great. He has no problem walking and has reached a high level of inner peace and harmony.

Practice:

If you think you are unhappy, try the following practice. In a comfortable place, simply accept your state of mind and allow it to be, just as it is, without resistance.

Make the following affirmation, connected with your innermost feeling: *"I am letting it be, I am allowing it to be as it is"*.

(If there is real acceptance, what you call unhappiness will disappear).

Finally, express your hope that this meditation will bring benefits to all beings without exception.

Story:

"People are unwilling to give up their jealousy and worries, their resentment and guilt, because these negative emotions are their "jabs" that make them feel alive," said the master.

And he gave this example:

"A mailman rode his bicycle through a field as a shortcut. Halfway through it, a bull noticed him and started chasing after him. In the end, after great difficulty, the man managed to reach safety.

"That was a close one, huh?" said someone who had been watching. "Yes," responded the mailman. "Same as every day".

Anthony de Mello

Chapter 40: Multiple sclerosis: the symbol of extreme perfectionism

"Disease is the effort made by nature to cure man".

Carl G. Jung

"Disease is the conflict between the personality and the soul".

Dr. Bach

"Disease is the healing hand of God".

Kalu T.

At the age of just 30, Gisela was diagnosed with multiple sclerosis. She had always lived in torment, gripped by fear and insecurity, and she felt great resentment and guilt, especially towards herself, because she had not accepted or forgiven many things about her past.

As a little girl she did not receive love from her parents and the only way she found to obtain it was to seek, like many people I have treated, perfection in all facets of life: as a student, as a daughter, as a friend, as a girlfriend, as a workmate...

She was always worrying about what others would think and she made great efforts to display a perfect image to others. She judged herself very harshly every time she made a mistake or did not live up to expectations (as judged by her own mental program). Her self-judgment was so cruel that it became a death sentence: playing the role of the accused, the judge and the executioner, she had attempted suicide more than once.

She suffered tremendously, she did not value herself, she constantly criticized herself, to the point of believing that she was an utterly worthless person. In our earliest sessions, she recognized that she did not love herself in the slightest: throughout her life, even in childhood, she had considered herself horrible. She had never been happy.

Without a doubt, Gisela was a textbook case of what many therapist friends of mine call "multiple troublosis" because of the symptom displayed by almost all people that have this disharmony: the feeling of being dissatisfied, of finding flaws in themselves, in others and in the world.

Her body had reacted to such a negative interior dialogue. All this fear caused neuronal disconnections and made her vitality fall to extreme lows. The right half of her body was losing sensitivity, she had lesions in the left hemisphere of her brain and she had great difficulty walking. Some doctors told her she would end up in a wheelchair.

She was so full of fears that she had become trapped by her negativity and mental toxicity. I asked her a question that was really hard for her to answer. I would even say that she avoided having to answer it:

—Which do you prefer? Being perfect or being healthy?

We talked about how absurd it is to seek perfection in a world in which there is no such thing (at least as we rationally understand this term). I suggested that she swap this perfectionism that caused her so much suffering for the concept of *excellence*... That way she could enjoy the process of growth and development, based on humor, joy and affection. She could improve herself while allowing herself to be spontaneous and to make mistakes, so necessary for learning and moving forward in any realm of life.

Imagine a basketball game. Before the players run onto the court, a group of depressed and poorly-coiffed cheerleaders appear, dragging their feet and saying:

—Why even bother playing if you always lose! You guys are terrible! You're no good for anything!

What attitude would the players have when the game started? Of course, this scenario never happens. No matter how low the team's classification is, its cheerleaders always shout its name as if it was sure to win the game, although the actual chances of victory were very remote. Think about how often we act like these "toxic" cheerleaders... We have a project and we boo and jeer at ourselves and then are surprised that things don't turn out as we would like. So, I urged Gisela to become a better cheerleader, to love herself instead of beating up on herself.

She understood all this quickly. She even gave me a timid smile. We got to work: we had to generate love and confidence within her... To be more exact, the walls and barriers built with so much judgmentalism and negativity had to be torn down, because they were separating her from that love that has always been inside her. To achieve this, the first thing would be to re-establish a constructive and conciliatory dialogue with herself.

It was also important that she get rid of her obsession for controlling things and her need to receive approval from others. I showed her a few techniques that would help her achieve these aims and, I must say, the results were impressive: the episodes of paralysis ended and she remained symptom-free for a long time. In fact, just a few months later I bumped into her one night. She was dancing, happy and completely healthy.

A year and a half passed with no news from Gisela. Then one day I received a telephone call. It was her and she was in a state of anguish. She had had a very severe relapse that had left her bedridden. I asked her to describe what had happened. I would like to share what she told me, because it is a very illustrative example of the effects that fear can have on our body.

The afternoon of the relapse, Gisela had been eating pizza at a restaurant when she saw an acquaintance of hers. It was someone she knew from the meetings that she had attended months ago, for patients of multiple sclerosis.

—Are you insane? What are you doing eating pizza? —he asked her in alarm.

—I love pizza... What's wrong with that?

—What do you mean "what's wrong with that"? Don't you know that pizza is one of the forbidden foods for people who have multiple sclerosis? Here, this website talks about all the things you can't eat...

Gisela didn't know that there were "forbidden foods". So she used her cell phone to look at the website and was horrified to discover that most of the foods listed there were a regular part of her diet.

That very night she had her first relapse. When she told me what had happened, I recommended that she stop looking at those sites for information about her physical challenge, and that she simply keep living her normal life. And that's what she did. Three years have gone by and Gisela has had no more relapses.

What do the masters say?

When we are hard on ourselves we are causing an impact inside us that affects every single cell in our body, because we are sending resentment and anger to our inner being. It is like voluntarily drinking shot glasses of poison: when the body receives this toxic information, it launches an attack on itself, as if it wanted to make itself disappear.

The absence of love is a lottery ticket with a sure prize: sickness and experiences with the flavor of hospital food. Because love is the base of life and health, the absence of love causes a lethal disharmony in our body, mind, emotions and energy field. Negative beliefs about ourselves lead us to experience a state of constant pain and suffering.

The masters understand that the universe is infinitely abundant and unlimited. So, if you talk to yourself in negative or destructive terms, the universe will give you an abundance of negative or destructive situations to live through over and over again. But if you talk to yourself positively and lovingly, it will give you an abundance of positive and prosperous situations for you to enjoy to the fullest.

Attacking yourself is an attack on life. You will think that life is working against you but in fact life is simply reflecting the battle that you are waging against yourself. If there is peace inside you, there is certain to be peace around you as well.

The first step for healing an illness is accepting it and allowing it to be, because the purpose of the illness is to heal our mind, improve our attitude towards life and reconnect us with life.

The second step would be to change all those attitudes and emotions that caused the disease in us.

What do the masters do?

They take constant and compassionate care of the relationship and dialogue they have with themselves, always opting for a sense of humor.

They choose a state of calm and peace, because they understand that a mind in peace is equal to health. They know that there can be no health if our mind is at war.

They understand that the most important thing in life is to feel and generate love within ourselves and that therefore we must place top priority on maintaining good inner health and peace, so that we can keep generating value and love in the world.

If they see that certain attitudes are having an impact on their body and wellness, they correct them immediately. To do so, they ask their body: what are you trying to tell me with this ailment or physical disharmony? Importantly, they never use the word disease. Instead, they call it an opportunity or a challenge.

They understand that a sick mind generates sickness and is a magnet for misfortune.

They generate love within themselves, love that they can then project to the world.

They let go of internal resistances that prevent them from enjoying their inner silence.

They work on self-forgiveness, always connecting with their own innocence, understanding that everything that happens has a reason and that the reason is always beneficial for our inner growth.

What do the masters not do?

They do not judge or condemn themselves or others.

They do not drag the burden of the past with them; they live in the present.

They do not worry about the image that others have of them, because they know it is neither their business nor their responsibility.

They do not voluntarily pay attention to things that are toxic to the mind. They do not feel guilty. They do not hold on to painful situations of the past; they accept them and understand that things could not be any other way.

They do not nourish disease by viewing it with fear or resistance.

They do not take themselves too seriously.

Practice:

Seated in a meditation position, breathe in deeply at least three times, while saying the following:

"I am letting go of everything false that disconnects me from life. Those projections are not me, they are not real".

Focus your attention on your heart, on the spot between the two halves of your ribcage, and be aware of this spot for at least a few minutes.

For as long as you feel is necessary, make these affirmations as indicated. As you inhale: *"I accept myself, I forgive myself, I love myself".*

As you exhale: *"I let go of all my judgments and of my past".*

Then make the following affirmation three times: *"I am innocent. I am peace".* Afterwards, sit still and observe your body with awareness for several minutes.

To conclude, express your hope that the benefits of this meditation will reach all beings without exception.

Story:

There is a group of elderly women in the waiting room at a doctor's office. A friend of theirs walks in and they all say:

—Hello, Fefa! How are you? We haven't seen you around here for awhile!

—Sorry, ladies, I've been a little under the weather.

Manolo Vieira (a well-known comedian in the Canary Islands)

Chapter 41:
The four women and disease

"Those who are always worrying about something cannot enjoy the world".

Lao Tse

"All that we are is the result of what we have thought. If with an impure mind a person speaks or acts, suffering will pursue him. If with a pure mind a person speaks or acts, happiness will follow him like his never-departing shadow".

Buddha

I would like to share two experiences related to the issue of illness. They both show how illness is often used in a harmful way. It is quite tragic but in fact it happens all too often. There are people who use it as a hobby, as if their entire life revolved around the new ailment (whether real or imaginary) that appeared that day. Worse still, there are people who use illness as a tool to manipulate others; they see illness as a way to receive the attention or affection they do not receive when healthy.

While I was writing the book you are now holding, I was in the habit of going to a nearby café every morning to have a cup of tea and review my notes.

I never deliberately listen to the conversations held by other people in the same space as I am, but my attention was drawn by this group of four or five older women who were often there and whose conversations always revolved around illness: from the slightest ache all the way to unbearable anguish, and always eventually touching on the subject of death, viewed from the perspective of fear. More than a gathering of friends it seemed like a competition to see who had more illnesses, who had the worst misfortunes befalling to them, and who had the most relatives, friends and acquaintances who were suffering.

Every day they met to talk about the same things. As the months went by I observed how the anguish in their faces increased. Their illnesses, ailments and even the negative events that were supposedly happening to them were growing day by day, in both number and severity.

But one day a very curious situation arose: an older woman with a radically different air about her came into the café. Smiling happily, she went up to the bar and asked for some sandwiches to take away. The four women greeted her effusively.

—Maruchi! Long time no see!

—Hello! How are you all doing? —responded Maruchi with a smile from ear to ear.

—Well, here we are, yet another day —said one.

—You know, getting by —said another with a sigh.

—More of the same! —exclaimed the third, nodding her head.

—Oh, struggling, day after day. The things I could tell you... —the last one rushed to say in a crafty attempt to be the first to narrate, with all kinds of details, the most recent misfortune to beset her. But before launching into the topic, she quickly asked the rhetorical question —And how are you?

—Well, I'm busy enjoying myself, because life is short! —she answered.

—Yes, it is, Maruchi! You're as positive as ever! —replied our four horsewomen of the apocalypse.

—Sit down and join us —one of the women said, pointing to an empty chair.

Maruchi went up to the waiter, who was calling her from the bar, and picked up her order. While she was putting the change in her wallet she looked at the women affectionately and told them:

—Girls, don't take this personally, but I don't feel like talking about illnesses or calamities. So I think it's best for me to go. I hope you all have a great day.

And having said that, she went through the door, leaving the others in a bit of a state. I must say, from that day forward I noticed a big change in them. They no longer had illness and misfortune as their sole topic of conversation. Clearly, this Maruchi had had quite an impact on these women.

It is interesting to see how people hold on to pain and turn it into their favorite subject. The equation "thought + emotion = vibration" is applicable in this case as well. A person who thinks about nothing but disease and places so much importance on them that they become the only topic of conversation will produce a vibration that ends up attracting this type of distress into his or her life. This in turn reinforces the role of victim, creating a vicious circle that can be very hard to break, and in which people like this poison their own lives and that of others around them.

Let me tell you about another case that really caught my attention. A man who was very worried about his niece called my office and asked me to have a private session with her. At the age of just 33, the niece suffered from anxiety and severe pain in her chest, back and stomach. Her health had deteriorated to such a point that her whole family had moved to Lanzarote to take care of her. I agreed to look at the case. A big surprise came when the young woman came to my office for the appointment. Just as she came in the room in which I see patients, she said to me:

—Could you do just the minimum for me?

—Excuse me? —I responded in bewilderment.

—Yes, I mean, don't cure me entirely —she said.

—I don't understand. What do you mean? You don't want to get well? —I asked her.

—Well, you see, thanks to my illness, my entire family has come from Galicia to be with me. If I get completely cured, they will leave and I'll be on my own again.

Considering this situation, I decided to spend the hour and a quarter that the sessions usually last simply talking to her. When her uncle came back to pick her up, I told him that there was no charge. He just needed to have a sincere conversation with his niece. Some people, to get attention, affection or dedication, grab hold of their illness and keep it alive. Often we fear change more than we fear death itself. For this reason, some people feel genuine panic at the thought of accepting responsibility and taking the reins of their lives.

What do the masters say?

Your energy (and therefore your life) will move wherever you put your mind and your attention. So, making a habit of talking about negative or painful news will attract more of these experiences to your existence: your mind manufactures experiences and then you have them.

The Tibetan monk Kalu T. once told me: "when, instead of looking so hard for names of illnesses, you look for the names of flowers, you will be on the path of peace".

Sometimes we seek love from a place of fear. This generates suffering in both you and the people around you. A person who lives under the influence of a conflict-oriented mindset is always demanding attention, love and appreciation, and is often willing to pay any price, even his or her health.

Complaints are the poison that puts a stop to a possible life of joy, peace and harmony, because complaints inevitably turn you into a magnet of unhappiness and misfortune.

The masters, taking this issue to a deeper level, say that we have the potential of the Universe within us (because we are children of God). So, if we identify with suffering or with a story of pain, we put all that potential at the service of misery.

What do the masters do?

They understand that we have a great opportunity in our existence as humans and, therefore, they connect with life and gratitude, focusing always on where life is: the present.

They connect with their inner greatness.

They take responsibility and let go of any leftover victim mentality. They choose to live in health, connected to life.

They use the formula "whatever you resist will persist; whatever you complain about will stay, and whatever you love will heal".

They feel gratitude instead of complaining.

They talk about possibilities and not calamities. They love everything without exception.

What do the masters not do?

They do not find delight in distress or unhappiness.

They do not talk about what is "wrong" or about misfortunes, unless their idea is to solve them. They do not adopt the role of victim.

They do not find entertainment in illness.

They do not demand love at the cost of their health or wellbeing. They do not beg for attention or affection.

Practice:

When you wake up in the morning and right before going to sleep, spend a little time feeling thankful, really feeling the emotion of gratitude, for at least six things, people or beings that are in your life and that enhance your wellbeing.

If there is some type of distress inside you, or an illness, connect with how you feel, observe the space that is within your heart and state:

"I allow this experience to be just as it is, I understand that it is life speaking to me, telling me to return my mind to love".

"What is life trying to tell me through this experience? Whatever it is, I am willing to collaborate with it".

Patiently and kindly allow the answer to spring up in you from your innermost feelings. Finally, hope that the benefits of this meditation will reach all beings without exception.

Story:

Once, two children were skating on a frozen pond when a fissure opened in the ice and one of the children fell through, becoming trapped underneath the thick layer of ice. His friend quickly took off his skates and used them to hit the ice to try to break it up, but the skates broke instead. He didn't give up though and he started to hit the ice with his fists. He kept hitting until the ice broke and he was able to rescue his friend from certain death.

When the authorities and the rescue teams arrived, everyone was amazed at what he had done. They asked the child how he had managed to break through the ice with his own hands. They got no answer from him and it remained a mystery for a few days. Then an old man heard about what had happened and exclaimed:

—He could do it because there was nobody around to tell him that he wouldn't be able to do it!

Chapter 42:
Children and the absence of affection

"While we try to teach our children everything about life,
our children teach us what life really is".

Angela Schwindt

"We want to be happy even though we live
in a way that makes happiness impossible.

Saint Augustine

I remember a married couple from northern Spain that was desperately trying to find a solution for the apparently physical problem that their 11-year-old daughter had. The girl could not open her hands: they had seized up suddenly and inexplicably at the age of seven. It was as if her fists were constantly and involuntarily closed tight, making her upper extremities useless for an infinite number of tasks. The couple had heard about Tibetan therapies and sound therapy so they contacted me and decided to come to Lanzarote. Shortly after that first call they came to see me with Laura, a sweet girl who turned out to love the sound of the gongs and the Tibetan bowls (which she called "little cauldrons").

The parents were consumed with anguish. Up until that time, no doctor, psychologist or therapist had been able to give them a convincing explanation for their daughter's "illness" (and much less a solution).

After observing them for several minutes, I perceived that those closed fists concealed something much more subtle. So, first

I spoke with them in private and I must say I did not beat around the bush.

—Did you want to have a child? —I asked.

After looking at each other for a moment, they admitted that no, she had not been wanted. In fact, they had even thought of the baby as an inconvenience but had decided to have it anyway.

—Do you give her hugs and kisses? Do you play with her? Do you let her know how important she is to you? —I went on.

They answered no to all of my questions. They told me that somehow they had never really been devoted to her: that sensation of an unexpected annoyance that had come along, disrupting their life and forcing them to change their plans, prevented them from doing so. They had later had another child and she did not receive much affection either. But they said they were willing to do anything to help the girl recover mobility in her hands.

I told them that just like buying a violin does not make you a violinist, having children does not make you a parent. If they wanted their daughter to get better, they would have to show affection to her, as of NOW. Clearly, since she was not receiving the affection so necessary for a child, Laura was closing up.

—So, start giving her hugs and saying nice things to her! Spend more time with her! —I suggested.

They were quite moved by all this and decided to change their attitude that very day. Making the most of their time in Lanzarote, they went to the beach, they played in the waves and in the sand, they explored some of the fantastic spots that this island has to offer, all with their daughter. In the meantime, I did some sessions with her, using sound therapy and Tibetan energy therapies. I started to notice that the child smiled more often and I could tell that she was more relaxed.

At the end of the second week, during one of the sessions in which Laura was lying down, almost asleep, on the table, I saw that one of her fingers started to move. A moment later I saw that other fingers were also beginning to move, now in both hands. The girl gradually became aware of what was happening. I simply observed her reaction.

She lifted her hands up to about the level of her head. While she moved her fingers, all of which were now open, she laughed and cried at the same time.

—Jos (that's what she called me), bring me a marker and a piece of paper was the first thing she said.

I did so. I stood there, deeply affected, watching her draw like crazy: clouds, volcanoes, dolphins, children, airplanes, stars, suns... She was drawing non-stop for half an hour, sighing in happiness all the while.

We then gave each other a big hug and right after that the doorbell rang. It was her parents.

—How was today's session? —they asked me when I opened the door.

—Come see for yourself —I answered, inviting them into the therapy room.

There was nothing but laughter, tears and hugs. I stayed outside, on the other side of the door, thanking the Universe and wearing a big smile on my face.

When I said goodbye to Laura, I gave her a 7 metal Tibetan singing bowl, one of those "little cauldrons" that she liked so much. The next day, before catching the plane back home, the girl dropped by my house. She gave me a little piece of paper on which she had written some phrases that defined her new state and that she wanted to share with me. And it certainly is a beautiful thing to share:

"The sun is rising. I am alive and
I can pull my little sister's ears.
I can pet my Chihuahua.
Today I can draw, write and play!
Today I was given a little cauldron
that makes music and that I can play.
Today I can give hugs!
Thank you!
Laura

(In silence, allow yourself to simply feel)

Story:

My suffering is unbearable, somebody said. And the Master responded:

—The present is never unbearable. What makes you feel desperate is thinking about what will happen within the next five minutes or over the next five days. Stop living in the future!

Anthony de Mello

Chapter 43: Impermanence

"Do not dwell in the past, do not dream about the future,
concentrate the mind on the present moment".

Buddha

In May of 2005 I was busy getting ready for a trip to Japan. That month, while hurriedly doing all the things that had to be done before my departure, I ran into Mario, a good friend of mine whom I had not seen for quite some time. Mario and I used to do a lot of things together: we often met to go surfing, bike-riding or do some other outdoor activity. But over the last year or so I hadn't seen or heard from him. He was very glad we had bumped into each other and he explained that he had "gone missing" because he had been building himself a house. He was very happy because, after much work and dedication, he had finally finished it. He said he would love to show it to me and that, now that he had more time, we would revive our friendship. It sounded like a great plan to me and I told him that I would get in touch with him as soon as I returned from Japan. We agreed to get together at his house, which was sure to be incredible, in a month's time, when I came back from the country of the rising sun.

That month sped by and my visit to Japan was very interesting, full of beautiful, intense experiences. I came back full of energy and eager to see my friend and tell him about those thirty marvelous days abroad. I tried calling him again and again but always got the same result: "the phone you are calling has been turned off or is out of range". I spent at least two days trying to reach him but had no luck, so I called a mutual friend to ask if he knew what was going on.

You mean you haven't heard? —this friend said. —Heard what? —I asked.

What came next left me totally speechless.

—Three weeks ago Mario had a stroke. He passed away two days later.

Mario had just recently turned 30 years old.

How many times in our life do we postpone encounters we want to have? How many people do not know how important they are to us? How many important things do we fail to do or say, not realizing that our life is fragile and fleeting? It is of prime importance that we live every day to the fullest, as if it were the very last day of our life, because one day it will be.

(In silence, allow yourself to simply feel)

Story:

—Master, what is the secret to longevity?

—Very simple, all you have to do is: eat half as much, walk twice as much and laugh three times as much.

Chapter 44: Never too late

"Life is what happens to you while you're busy making other plans".

John Lennon

"Live as if you were going to die tomorrow.
Learn as if you were going to live forever".

Mahatma Gandhi

Sandra was 80 years old when we met. She lived consumed by fear, anguish, insecurity and guilt. She depended entirely on her daughters and granddaughters to do anything at all: she walked with a cane and was always besieged by doubts when undertaking any activity, so much so that she usually gave up on the idea and stayed home doing what a woman of that age is "supposed" to do: watch soap operas.

But Sandra did not like soap operas. She would have preferred to go to the beach, go out dancing, or sing... Too bad she was too old for all of that! And, anyway, nobody wanted to go with her.

One day during a private session she confided to me that she had been suffering insomnia and frequent panic attacks for some time. They were becoming so bad that sometimes she thought that all she wanted to do was die and put an end to it all.

We talked for a long time about how to manage the fears that plagued her, how to end her dependence on others and how to spend more time doing what she really loved. After two more sessions, something changed in Sandra.

Two weeks later, I noticed that she was dressed differently: she had gotten rid of her dull old-lady outfits and had renewed not just her wardrobe but also her driver's license. With her savings she bought a used car and started going to the beach by herself, she began attending painting classes, she went for walks with her friends, she went out to the country for picnics... she even went out dancing!

Her family was amazed at the new-found independence shown by grandma, who no longer spent her days watching TV and cooking for others. No, sir, she couldn't do that anymore. She had things to do. She was very busy... living her life! She was happily occupied (instead of *pre-occupied*), finally devoting more time to herself and also having enriching experiences with her great-grandchildren. It was quite a life!

One of her daughters told me that Sandra had gone through a complete metamorphosis. Her strength and joy were amazing.

The only thing that Sandra had done was rid herself of those absurd fears, of that silly concern about what other people would think, of her dependence on others, of her not wanting to be a bother...

Three years later, Sandra passed away. I will never forget the words she told me a month before leaving this world:

—José, in the last three years I have lived more than in my entire life before that.

(In silence, allow yourself to simply feel)

Story:

One day someone asked a teacher:

—What if I don't want to be happy? What if I prefer to be miserable?

The teacher responded:

—OK then, be miserable if that's what makes you happy!

Chapter 45: Events are neutral; it all depends on how you relate to them emotionally

"Complaints are the language of defeat".

Frank Crane

"Havelock Ellis: 'The place where optimism flourishes the most is in the lunatic asylums'.
"Albert Einstein: 'Well, I would rather be an
optimistic lunatic than a sane pessimist.'

Alice Calaprice (in *Quotable Einstein*)

Several years ago something happened while I was on my way from Madrid to San Diego. I was thrilled because this was to be my first visit to the United States. When the plane arrived in Chicago, where I had a layover of about two and a half hours, all passengers had to go through a very thorough immigration check: after some very long lines there was a row of agents who checked passports, asked questions, took fingerprints of both hands, photographed us...

I simply smiled and told myself that it was *"their way"* of doing things, their way of protecting their borders. So, I accepted it and continued to enjoy the excitement I felt at finally being in that great country.

Next to me, in the same line, there was a woman travelling with a friend. The two of them complained non-stop about how horribly unpleasant it was to have to wait in a line that seemed to never end. Clearly, they were not accepting the situation they were in and their resistance to it caused them to suffer, because it triggered their victim-oriented mindset.

When we finally reached the head of the line, all of us went through the same checkpoint. It was my turn first: with a big smile on my face, I said hello to the agent who, after asking me the pertinent questions, kindly allowed me to go through.

Our friend, with a bad attitude and an even worse expression on her face, went next: using a scornful tone, she barely deigned to answer the questions posed by the agent, who, in this situation, decided to have her bags inspected and make her wait in an adjacent room. The two women would miss their connecting flight and have to wait until the next day because all other flights were full. When I left the area to board the plane that would take me to San Diego, they were still complaining that they had been treated like criminals, exclaiming "if we'd known this would happen we never would have come here".

If we look at all this in perspective, we can see that perhaps it was in fact their negative attitude and refusal to cooperate that brought about the predicament.

Some masters say things along these lines: "*to trip and fall on the path is normal; but to become addicted to the rock that you trip over... that is something else!*"

(In silence, allow yourself to simply feel)

Story:

There were two monks who lived together for forty years and never argued. Not even once. One day, one of them said to the other: "Don't you think it's about time for us to argue, at least once?"

The other monk said: "All right, let's do it! What shall we argue about?"

"What about this loaf of bread?" responded the first monk. "Fine, let's argue about the bread. How do we do it?" asked the other monk.

The first monk said: "That bread is mine, it belongs to me".

The second monk replied: "Well, if that's the way it is, then take it!"

Anthony de Mello

Chapter 46:
The monk who danced salsa

"Those who do not laugh have learned nothing".

Lao Tse

In the late 1990s I met a Tibetan lama whom we will call T. He seemed like a really extraordinary person, with interesting ideas about spiritual evolution: to him, the idea was not to adopt the role of a saint (which in fact is nothing but the other side of the coin of a conflict-oriented mindset; an ego clamoring to be considered special), but rather to experience the changes that take place as a natural process, feeling comfortable and always being kind to oneself.

At a week-long workshop that T. was teaching, something curious happened that perfectly illustrates this way of understanding spirituality. It was the middle of August and the weather was very hot. During the lunch break, a group of about twenty of us went, along with T., to a restaurant. There the waiter asked us what we would like to drink while waiting for our food. No doubt conditioned by the presence of the lama, we all asked for the same sort of thing: water, juice, herb tea... But when it was T's turn to order, he smiled, spread his arms wide and said:

——I want a beer this big!

We all started laughing, including the lama, who simply said:

——Remember, friends, the middle path.

Another night, when we had finished our workshop activities, someone suggested that we go out dancing. So, after dinner, we offered to take the lama to the house in which he was staying so that he could get some rest... To this he responded with a smile and the words:

——But why? I want to go dancing too!

So we all went to a small dance club near the restaurant, and the lama surprised us again: he danced salsa better than anyone in the place!

He confessed that he had learned from a monk of Cuban extraction who had lived at the monastery for three and a half years.

Once again I had before me a great teacher helping me break limiting beliefs!

Practice:

Seated in a meditation position, connecting deeply with how you feel, make the following affirmations as indicated.

As you inhale: *"My mind is like crystal clear water"*.

As you exhale: *"It reflects everything just as it is"*.

Repeat as many times as you feel is necessary. This practice will give you greater mental clarity.

Afterwards, express your hope that this practice will benefit all beings without exception.

Apache blessing:

"May the sun bring you new energy by day.

May the moon softly restore you by night. May the rain wash away your worries.

May the breeze blow new strength into your being.

May you walk gently through the world and know its beauty all the days of your life".

Chapter 47:
Watering the seeds of power in others

"Man's heart is a musical instrument, it contains wonderful music. The music is asleep but it is there, waiting for the right moment to be performed, expressed, sung and danced. And it is through love that that moment will come".

Rumi

Several years ago I met an incredible person in Sydney. His name was Woong Sun An, but his Western friends called him A.J. He was a budding photographer, aged about 22, from Korea. At that point in his life he had been travelling the world for some time but was under a lot of pressure from his parents to start working. What the job was didn't matter. They just wanted him to find regular employment that would allow him to live a "normal" life and prove that he was "a hardworking man". Although his passion and dream profession was photography, his family had been urging him to "give up that nonsense and come back to Korea once and for all".

He had even started to believe that they were right. But before going back to his home country to begin a boring, pre-determined existence, he had decided to try his luck "down under" and spend a few months in Australia with his camera as his only companion. You never know what might happen...

He worked at whatever jobs came his way, earning enough to survive for awhile and keep travelling, taking pictures all over Australia. He lived from hand-to-mouth but such a situation, far from worrying him, made him very happy.

We started talking about photography, painting and other artistic experiences... And he showed me a selection of his photos. They were true works of art, oozing with sensitivity, magic and inspiration.

New Year's Eve was approaching. I asked him what he planned to do for the big night and he said he would try to take some pictures of Sydney Harbor. If he was lucky enough to find a good spot, that is. The best way would be to shoot from the water, in one of those special boats that take people out to the bay for New Year's Eve... His face lit up just thinking about it. But, of course, a ticket on one of those boats, on the night that the Sydney sky fills with light and color, was totally beyond his budget.

I was not exactly overflowing with money either. But the next day I went to the port and, without thinking twice, I bought two tickets. Each one of them cost approximately 400 Australian dollars. I asked him to meet me at the port at 2 p.m. on the 31st.

When I saw him, I walked towards him and, with a big smile, I showed him the tickets. He could not believe it. Jumping for joy, he said over and over again he didn't know how he would ever be able to pay me back or return such a nice gesture.

——Friend, you don't have to return the gesture and much less pay me back. I know that one day you will be a great photographer, an artist that will bring beauty to the world and to other beings. If you want, we can do something symbolic: when you have your first international exhibition, you can invite me to the opening.

His eyes shined with emotion. He said it was wonderful that someone had so much confidence in him and his art. At that moment he became more committed than ever to persist in his dream of becoming a photographer.

The boat ride in Sydney Bay was marvelous and that unforgettable New Year's Eve was captured forever in our hearts and in the amazing pictures taken by A.J., who couldn't stop saying how happy and inspired he felt.

(In silence, allow yourself to simply feel)

Story:

Once upon a time there were three caterpillars who knew nothing about their future life as butterflies. Their names were: Pessimist, Realist and Optimist. The time for their metamorphosis was approaching and they started to feel the first signs...

Their formerly-voracious appetites were smaller and they had less and less mobility. Soon they found themselves building a cocoon that enveloped them, separating them from the familiar world, from the security of their normal lives. In the darkness, the mystery of their future came to mind and they all had different reactions:

Pessimist thought to himself fearfully that the end of his life was surely near and he said goodbye to the good times.

Realist cheered himself up by saying that it was probably temporary and that sooner or later things would go back to normal.

Optimist felt that whatever it was that was happening to him might be the opportunity to fulfill his most cherished dream: to be able to fly. And he made the most of the darkness to perfect his dreams.

When the three cocoons opened, they revealed three equal, yet different, situations ...

Pessimist was a beautiful butterfly but... he was dead. He had died of fright!

Realist was also a beautiful butterfly... but, despite his new form, he started dragging himself along the ground just as he always had. He thanked heaven that things were the same as ever.

Optimist, as soon as he saw the light of day, started looking for his wings... When he saw them, his heart bursting with joy, he took to the air and said thank you to the world, spreading his happiness to the entire forest.

Carlos González Pérez

Chapter 48:
Masters who ask life for challenges

"Suffering teaches nothing; it is only an indicator that you are disconnected from life and from what you really are".

Master J. Kim

"If you cling to happiness it is the same as clinging to suffering, but you don't realize it. When you hold on to happiness it is impossible to throw away the inherent suffering. They're inseparable that way.

Ajahn Chah

At the age of just twenty I saw something that really grabbed my attention. It was some elderly lamas doing a special type of meditation... At least that is what it looked like to me. And when I found out what it was, it turned out that my intuition was right: what the lamas were doing was something out of the ordinary, something I had never heard of before that day.

One day, during a retreat, I asked one of them to explain what that unusual practice was all about. He told me that they were "simply" asking that the Universe give them, in their next reincarnation, a difficult situation, such as being born into very tough family circumstances, so that they could reach awakening sooner and thus move further along their spiritual path.

I could not quite understand this, or, to be more exact, I had a hard time digesting this concept. So the monk went on, quoting an old

Chinese proverb and making reference to conditioned happiness: *"The best way to hurt your enemy is to wish him one hundred years of happiness"*.

You see —he explained when he saw the bewilderment in my face—, if I am reborn into a place where everything is given to me, I will never feel the impulse that leads me to awakening. I will believe the world I see and so I will not take up the teachings again... This is because there is an essential question that opens the doors of understanding for us and it is: "Is there an alternative to this suffering?" Although what happened with Siddharta Gautama Buddha is another possibility: even though he was born into princely circumstances and had everything he could ever want or need, his great dissatisfaction prompted him to go out in search of awakening. You must realize that everything that to the ego seems like suffering is but an illusion for the lucid mind. Thus, when I awaken, I will understand that what I first took to be suffering was really just a means to put me on the path to awakening.

Some time later, I met other masters who worked with shamanic tools from the ancient Tibetan philosophy known as Bon. In their practices, they asked the Universe to send them challenges (what we normally call "problems") that would allow them to continue cleansing, letting go of resistance, and giving their mind back to love and comprehension. One funny thing about this is that when the masters ask for these challenges, they do not often receive them, or they receive them only insofar as they are absolutely necessary to purify some aspect of that master's life.

An example of this is Mr. Díaz, who was always asking life for challenges but never getting any. And then one day he began to feel intense pain in his side. He went to the hospital and the necessary tests were performed. He was diagnosed with liver cancer. It was almost if he had won the lottery. Mr. Díaz smiled cheerfully and enthusiastically thanked the doctor, who, upon witnessing such a strange reaction, spoke with extreme tact:

—Yes, this is something that can be quite difficult to assimilate... If you like, we will put you in touch with a psychologist...

—Thank you very much but that won't be necessary —responded Mr. Díaz. —What I would like is for you to see me again in one month. And to have all the tests done again at that time.

The disconcerted doctor mentioned again the possibility of seeing a psychologist and tried to tell him how urgent it was to start

the conventional treatment given to all oncology patients.

But Mr. Díaz kindly refused and left the doctor's office feeling truly glad, giving thanks to the Universe, because he understood that life was speaking to him through that ailment. He knew he still had some psychological issues from the past that needed to be healed, and a phrase from his master Kalu T. came to mind: *"disease is the healing hand of God"*. And that is what he had to do, continue to heal his mind, and especially his past.

Mr. Díaz never even treated his liver, he only worked on the emotional causes that were behind it. One month later he returned to the same doctor and, as they had agreed on the day of the diagnosis, the tests were repeated... The result was remarkable: not a sign of the tumor. The doctor was so astounded that he actually wondered if Mr. Díaz was perhaps some sort of magician. That very same day he became one of Mr. Díaz' students.

The message of this chapter is not that we must suffer in order to evolve... On the contrary: if you suffer it is because you are resisting the natural flow of life and are perceiving the world with the wrong mindset, using a conflict-oriented program. I can tell you now that there is nothing to be learned from suffering all the time or from generating distress for yourself. The only thing that can be learned from all that suffering is that you are not on the right path; in other words, feeling that way may help you decide to change the direction of your life, moving towards peace and towards the search for what you really are, with an attitude of humility and receptiveness.

Practice:

In close connection with your heart and inner feelings, make the following affirmations:

"Today I will let go of control and release all of my resistances".

"Today I will allow the Universe to do as it will, collaborating with life's flow with full acceptance and joy".

"I will stop fighting the way things are and I will be one with life".

"Thank you, thank you, thank you".

Story:

—Why are you always praying? asked the master.

—Because prayer lessens the burden on my mind.

—Unfortunately, that's what prayer tends to do...

—And what's wrong with that?

—It prevents you from seeing who put the burden there in the first place, replied the master.

Anthony de Mello

Chapter 49:
Releasing burdens and resistances

"If you bring forth what is within you, what you bring forth will save you.
If you do not bring forth what is within you, what you do not bring forth will destroy you.

Gospel of St. Thomas

"He who walks softly goes far".

Chinese proverb

As we have discussed in earlier chapters, behind all disharmony and illness there is an emotional cause disconnected from love.

A few months ago I had an interesting case that confirmed, once again, this great truth. It was a woman who had gained 130 pounds for no apparent reason. She had gone from weighing 130 to 260 pounds without knowing why. And try as she might, she could not take all that extra weight off. She was baffled: she told me she did not overeat and she did not lead an especially sedentary life.

She came to see me out of desperation. She felt guilty and sad about this situation, which was causing many problems in her life and creating limitations at work. Our conversation provided some clues that helped me discover something very interesting: the emotional cause of her physical state.

Some time before this sudden weight gain, her mother, upon whom she was very emotionally dependent, had fallen ill and, shortly thereafter, passed away. She had not been able to take care of her mother during her illness and she now lived in a torment of guilt. She felt very anxious and could not come to terms with her mother's death. I asked her how long it had been since she gained the extra weight. She told me it had been three and a half years, exactly the time since her mother had died. But the big surprise came afterwards. I wanted to know how much her mother had weighed... She responded that her mother had always weighed about 130 pounds. How amazing! We could almost say that this woman had her mother inside her, emotionally and energetically speaking.

To help her give up these negative emotions once and for all, I recommended her to go to the cemetery and say a sincere goodbye to her mother. She did what I asked and once she had released all that guilt and resistance, she started losing all those extra kilos and soon returned to her normal weight. And more importantly, she began to feel truly free and light.

Practice:

Observe your thoughts as if they were outside of you, letting them drift by. Do not hold on to them or pay much attention to them. Allow them to flow freely and observe them as if you were a big open space, like the sky with clouds floating through it.

Make this a daily practice, starting with a few minutes and increasing the time gradually as you feel more and more comfortable doing it.

At the end of each meditation, hope that the benefits of this meditation will reach all beings without exception.

Story:

"If you are looking for God, you are looking for ideas... And you are ignoring reality," said the teacher.

And he told the story of a monk who complained about the cell he had been assigned: "I wanted a cell from which to contemplate the stars, but this one has a stupid tree in front of it, blocking my view...".

However, looking at that tree was precisely how the cell's previous occupant had reached illumination".

Anthony de Mello

Chapter 50:
People telling their own stories

"We are all seeking the summit of the holy mountain, but shall not our road be shorter if we consider the past a chart and not a guide?"

Khalil Gibran *Sand and Foam*

Before finishing this book I want to share some texts written by real people who have experienced the blessings of these tools in their lives. They have been kind enough to let me share their stories with everyone who reads the book.

Juan Tomás González

Words cannot describe how I felt during my first session of Reiki and Tibetan energy therapies. It is something that has to be experienced. To tell the truth, at the beginning I wasn't very receptive. My problems had led me to try various alternative therapies, but none had worked. However, a little voice inside me told me that this was going to be different. And it certainly was!

Perhaps the good vibrations and the trust that I have always felt around the person who urged me to go is what made me finally take the step to go see José Antonio that afternoon. I had nothing to lose and now I can say that I had a lot to gain.

I had had a stroke and I went to the appointment in a wheelchair because I could not keep my balance while walking (or so I thought). Also, I had a vision dysfunction that made me see double.

The person who received me was youthful and pleasant and it immediately seemed that I had known him all my life. That was the feeling he transmitted. When the session started, I closed my eyes and let myself go. I started to feel calm and relaxed. At one point I felt a sudden heat in my chest but very soon I went back to a state of relaxation. After a while he said to me: "Open your eyes, Juan. Stand up and walk, because you are not afraid anymore". I stared at him but did as I was told. I started to walk; I could follow him without any help and with perfect balance, just like I used to (prior to the stroke).

I will remember that day for the rest of my life. I left the office pushing the wheelchair from behind, not sitting in it. After several weekly sessions I also stopped seeing double. Incredible! I, who had been very skeptical about all these energy-based therapies and, more specifically, about José Antonio, am now convinced that there are other ways. I keep going to sessions of this type of therapy because I find that it makes me feel better than ever. As an aside, since then my doctor calls me "a little miracle".

Carmen Delgado Hernández (Nenena)

That night I made the firm decision to take my own life. I had been thinking about it for some time but hadn't decided how to do it. The easiest thing to do would be to take a bunch of pills. I had been taking anti-depressants all my life, so that method was quite handy. But what would happen if my children found me too soon? What would they go through afterwards? More suffering, more pain and the fear that I would try again? No, pills were not a good option. It had to be something certain, with no chance of failure; there would be no turning back.

I waited for everyone to go to sleep and at about three in the morning I got in my car and went to Mirador del Río, a lookout point near where I live. I planned to drive off the cliff. I still don't know where that determination came from. I, who had agoraphobia, who was afraid to leave the house by myself, now had a clear objective: to put an end to my life.

I remember feeling a deep sadness. The tears made it hard to see the road. Even so, I felt more and more certain as I approached my destination. That night it would all be over.

When I was very close to the top, about 300 yards, a dense cloud appeared before me, reducing the visibility to practically zero. A few minutes later it had surrounded the car. I couldn't see anything so I pulled over to the shoulder to wait. Thoughts were pummeling my brain. I couldn't stop crying, and in my chest I felt a big knot squeezing my heart and making it hard to breathe. I thought about my children, about the pain that this would cause them, but I was sure that it was the best for everyone. I had already caused too much suffering with my frequent depressions.

My family had always come first in my life: my children, my husband, my dog, my house... and then me. In fact, at that moment, while I was waiting for the cloud to dissipate, I decided to jump without the car. That way my children could still use it.

But the cloud didn't want to dissipate. It looked like it was there to stay. Minutes passed, then hours, until I finally saw a faint light on the horizon. Suddenly, as if somebody up above were blowing air over me, the cloud moved aside and revealed the most beautiful sunrise I have ever seen. While I contemplated the beauty of that moment, lost in myself, a thought suddenly came to me and took over my entire mind: "God doesn't want me to go yet".

If God wanted me to stay, despite the suffering, I would stay. The tears didn't stop, in fact they fell with even more intensity than before. I stayed there without moving, incapable of starting the car. Hours went by, until the sun's heat started to bother me. It was 11 a.m. by the time I got home. Everyone was very worried; they thought something had become of me. I didn't tell them what had happened that night until months later.

My life moved along the same as ever, with my ups-and-downs, my anxiety, my panic attacks, my sadness... Until, some time thereafter, someone recommended that I attend a Reiki in Solidarity event. I didn't go out very often and in fact it took a huge effort for me to break that habit and decide to go. But I did it: I surprised myself and stepped out of my usual routine. As soon as I got there I found myself in a room filled with people. Too many people, I remember thinking at the time. Among them, there was one person who particularly caught my attention, a wonderful creature who spoke to me with love and shared some keys that turned out to be very useful. Something had changed.

I was firmly on my way to becoming a new person when I got home that day. On August 4, 2012 I started learning Usui Reiki. At that moment my life made a 180° turnaround. All my life I had taken anti-depressants, lots of them and in high doses. I took 8-10 a day usually, and even in my better moments I took two. Since that day I haven't taken a single pill. But the most important thing is that I am happy. Every day I thank God for putting that cloud on that mountaintop and for making me cross paths with my teacher, that angel who helped me save my life and who has given me back the joy that I unfortunately lost way too soon.

Now I realize that, even though life has given me some beautiful moments, I was always anchored to the past. I have had times, days, years, that I felt very depressed, sad, angry... I was angry with my coworkers, my family, with the world, and with myself. In addition, I felt the burden of all the pain I was causing my children and my husband with my constant bitterness!

At this point I have completed two levels of Usui and of Tibetan energy techniques and I feel like a totally different woman. I feel this great love, towards everything and everyone. Even though I have had to leave behind certain people who were hurting me, because they were hindering my development and my happiness, I have tasted the sweetness of forgiving and I hope, from the bottom of my heart, that these people also find the happiness, love and peace that I have been fortunate enough to experience.

Today I look neither towards the future nor back at the past, I just live day by day, thankful to be part of this wonderful family with which I feel so at ease.

Now I enjoy every sunrise, my marvelous travelling companion (my husband), my children, my baby grand-daughter, my job, nature, the gifts that life brings me every day.

I am telling my story because it might help other people who are going through complicated situations... I have been there. I truly hope they can find the strength they need and experience the happiness I now have, that they can enjoy all those small but wonderful moments that are within our reach every day, but that often go unnoticed.

These days I never tire of giving thanks because, although it is true that I have suffered, I have also managed to reach the place I am now and to feel what I feel now. And that is a lot. Thank you, cloud. Thank you, José Antonio. Thank you, husband. Thank you, life.

Carmen Hernández (nurse)

The first of these experiences occurred just a few weeks after completing the second level of Usui Reiki. I am a nurse at the General Hospital of Arrecife and that day a relative of mine was brought into the operating room for a planned C-section. I was standing at the door, observing. All of a sudden, complications arose. It happened very quickly: the baby girl stopped breathing and the doctors tried to resuscitate her, but they could do nothing for her and the baby went into cardiopulmonary arrest. From where I was standing, I heard a voice telling me: "You are light. You need to go inside". I was watching the pediatrician try to get a heartbeat but the baby didn't respond. I went inside and started sending Reiki, paying no attention to what was going on around me; all I was concerned about was that baby. I did the "Cho Ku Rei" symbol and, placing my hands on the tiny body, I projected to her chest and heart area. The baby started to cry immediately and that got her breathing. Even though she had been in cardiac arrest for almost five minutes, she is perfectly healthy and has shown no aftereffects.

The second experience happened some time after that. Although I had started the shift in Intensive Care that day, for a number of reasons I ended up in the delivery room. We were informed that a woman in labor was coming in to have some tests done (it turned out to be a friend of mine who was having her second child). She was examined and the diagnosis was "meconium aspiration syndrome". Meconium is the first intestinal discharge from newborn babies and normally it is stored in the intestine until the baby has been delivered. But sometimes (usually because of intrauterine distress) it is expelled into the amniotic fluid before the birth. If this happens, the baby runs the risk of serious respiratory problems during labor. In the case of my friend, the baby, still in the womb, had entered cardiopulmonary arrest. The midwife and I started sending Reiki and we got the heart beating again. We then went into the operating room for an emergency

C-section. Besides the meconium, we found other problems as well: vagal syndrome, bradycardia and two cord entanglements. The doctors tried to resuscitate her but they could not get her going. Then the pediatrician said this to me:

—You wake her up. You know how to do it.

So I went up to the baby and started sending her Reiki. It seemed to have an effect, but every time I stepped away, the little girl relapsed, so the pediatrician and the midwife told me to stay by her side. We went up to the pediatrics ward. There, a chest X-ray revealed that she had inhaled meconium-contaminated amniotic fluid. This fluid is very dangerous because it can cause pneumonia in a newborn. So I was sending Reiki all day long. Although she was getting better, she still had trouble breathing. The next day I tried a method I had learned from the Tibetan energy techniques; it consists of taking away all the excess negative energy. A few seconds later, the baby started vomiting and expelling the liquid from her lungs. Some more tests were done and the pediatrician told me she was completely cured. She has had no aftereffects and is now growing and gaining weight just like any other baby.

I feel very fortunate to have these marvelous tools that are bringing so much to my life and to those around me, and I thank the Universe for them every day.

Ibán Bermúdez Betancor

Hello. My name is Ibán and I am 32 years old. Seven months ago I was diagnosed with cancer and now I am grateful for having had it. What happened during this time to make me feel this way? "I don't know" is my answer... But let's take this step by step and see if we can make any sense out of it...

In August of last year I was admitted to the hospital because, at a routine work-related medical check-up, certain anomalies in my body were detected. The anomalies had to be analyzed to rule out that disease that so frightens me... or that used to frighten me. The days prior to the tests were absolutely horrendous: being worried about something, not knowing if I had it or not (as it turns out, I did) completely paralyzed my life and made the wait unbearable. I was consumed by anguish and desperation... waiting for the dreaded news to arrive.

Of the days I spent in the hospital I remember only being afraid: afraid of the doctors, afraid of being alone, afraid of hearing what I did not want to hear, afraid of dying, absolute panic at the thought of not living any longer...

And then the big news came; I was told that I had cancer. The doctors had previously ruled out another type of cancer, which, according to them, has no cure. That is what I thought, too, although later I learned that everything has a solution. But that would come later and I don't want to get ahead of myself.

So, holding the diagnosis, Hodgkin's lymphoma, in my hand, I left the hospital feeling relieved. However, I felt relief because I was leaving the hospital, getting out of that place where I had felt so much fear. Once out, I couldn't think, I was incapable of thinking about the future. All I wanted was to go on living, to have the chance to live again. I wanted to have the good fortune of being born again, the way many people feel when they defeat cancer.

I told all this to a friend of mine, a friend I often call "little angel" and she considered my attitude to be very positive. She recommended that I attend a Reiki session because she had the feeling that it would help me; it would be yet another tool with which to deal with what was ahead of me. And I was willing to do anything in order to get that second chance at life, so I accepted her suggestion without a moment's hesitation. That is how I met José Antonio Manchado, my teacher, although since I know he doesn't like to be called a teacher, I will call him friend from now on, because that is what he has been and still is to me.

At my very first session with him, everything started to change, although at the time I was not aware that everything was going to change. I remember the first time that I went to see him: sitting face to face, looking into each other's eyes and him wanting to hear my entire story, wanting to know what had happened, why I had decided to go see him. I didn't know a thing about Reiki (and I probably still know nothing) but I found in him just what I needed: a person who transmitted hope and who surprised me by saying that diseases have emotional causes, that the treatment might cure the symptoms but that the emotional causes also needed to be healed because otherwise they would come back, in one way or another. "Cancer has an emotional cause," he said over and over again... And I asked him how to find that cause, because I wanted to heal it. "By listening to yourself you will find the answer; by connecting with your innermost feelings and your heart, you will know for sure," was his response.

Another phrase he shared with me and that in the end became my favorite was "cancer is an opportunity that life gives you to bring out the very best version of yourself". With a headline like that, nothing much else needs to be said. So I listened to the phrase and tucked it away inside me, although at that moment, at that very moment, I didn't think it was as important as it would turn out to be later.

"Can I go outside, and to places where lots of people are?" That was another question I asked, because my family was over-protecting me almost to the point of putting me inside a bubble and isolating me from the world, so that, according to them, I wouldn't get even sicker, since my defenses were probably very low. "Of course you can go out! Lead a normal life, feel the life in you. Those are nothing but limiting beliefs that people impose on you, beliefs that translate into fear. If you want to go out, you can". And so I started living, or I kept on living, not letting people scare me and always believing in myself, feeling alive. And I must say that during the entire treatment ("beauty treatment" as I like to say) I did not get sick a single time. Everyone around me came down with the awful flu that people said was going around... Everyone except me! Despite my supposedly

low defenses!

I remember another occasion, two or three Reiki sessions later, in which José Antonio told me that when I accepted the process I was going through, when I felt that what I was living through was going to be good for me, the cancer would disappear, because it was really just a symbol, a sign that something in me had to change.

So, with all those tools and many more that I learned along the way, I started to experiment, to search, to feel, to move forward in life, while leading the most normal life possible. And one day, I don't know exactly which, I was surprised to discover that I felt thankful for having that cancer. That day, I don't know how or why, I felt grateful, maybe because I was discovering a new version of myself that I hadn't seen before. Over the next few days I started sharing that sentiment with others, even at the risk of them thinking I was insane... First I shared it with those I felt might understand me better. Then I shared more openly, with everyone, because that is what I felt I had to do. And the more I said it, the more certain I was of what I felt, the more grateful I was for going through this process and finding out what I really was, what I really wanted to be.

Before I thought I was happy but now, knowing what I know now, I realize that I wasn't happy before this happened. Now I can truly say that I am happy, that I feel peace. And that from now on I want to be happy. That is what I want, to be happy. How will I achieve it? By listening to myself, by feeling that what I am doing is what I really want to do.

I knew that I had healed my emotional cause when I started to feel peace. During the entire process I felt a lot of different fears, primarily the fear that I would not overcome the illness, but those fears did not stop me from moving forward. My starting point was my desire to live and all of this taught me to live, to live in peace. And each step I took was a victory and a source of personal satisfaction. I was able to work, I was able to play paddleball, my favorite sport (although with my left hand instead of my right), I was able to travel, to overcome my aversion to smells, I could even be proud of my hair, which not only did not fall out but even started to grow before the end of my "beauty treatments". I was able to deal with a lot of things and, despite the difficulties and the bad times, I kept on saying that I was grateful for having had cancer, because now I really was happy, a happy madman.

When I received the results and learned that it was all over, that I was completely healthy, I did not have the feeling of being reborn. That is what I would have expected before, because I thought my life would stop until I received the good news... But that's not the way it was, because I never stopped living, in the end what I did was go on living my life. They say that I understood the symbolism of cancer, they say that I trusted myself and all those who helped me (and there were many) and they say I managed to overcome my challenge because I reconnected with life. How did I do it? I don't know!

www.ibanconbb.blogspot.com.es

Jezabel Suarez

What is a miracle? According to my teacher, it is the deactivation of a limiting belief that says "it's impossible". There are times when something that seems impossible becomes possible... The universe is such that many situations arise simultaneously or in alternation. This brings a result...either a good one or a bad one. But... what if you do not judge it? The lesson to be learned is this; the result is neither good nor bad, it just is.

I also believe that we are heard by the universe... What message do you send out, hope or desperation? What is the usual constant factor inside you? Do you complain or express gratitude? Do you conform or do you pursue your dreams? Do you let yourself become trapped by fear or do you listen to it with love?

This is yet another story among the many disease processes that are taking place or have already taken place. But it is the story of the disease and healing process of my father; and it is also the story of my own disease and healing process as a daughter. I am now 30 years old. For the past six I have been an oncology nurse. My work has allowed me to see and share many processes of disease, hope and recovery, and also processes of inner conflict and of death. Two years ago, motivated mostly by my desire to comfort those who suffer, I began experimenting with energy through Reiki, and it turned out to be a very powerful and useful tool, as I will explain below.

And then cancer, which I already knew too well, reared its head once again... This time in my father's body.

On December 31, 2010, my father became jaundiced (yellow skin and mucous membranes, due to a hepatic obstruction). In Spain the custom is for families to celebrate the arrival of the New Year by eating 12 grapes, one for each month. My family rang in 2011 at the hospital. I realized then how often I had failed to be grateful for the New Year, taking for granted those annual celebrations in which my family gathered and our health was good.

After several days of tests the doctors told us that the jaundice was probably due to an obstruction of the biliary conduits. On the Twelfth Day of Christmas —traditionally a day of gift-giving in Spain— we cried when we found out the reason for the obstruction: a tumor. How absurd it was to be unwrapping presents! Needless to say, material items did nothing to console us. That was the day we really started to beg the universe to save my father. A polarity of sentiments took hold of me and my family, a mix of hope and desperation.

The fear I felt was aggravated by the mental codes that had been reinforced by years of working with oncology patients. I turned to Internet to get information about prevalence, prognosis, treatments, statistics of various types... As if this kind of information would make me feel any better! In fact, it just added to my fears and doubts: instead of concentrating on his healing process and my own, all I was doing was strengthening the idea that there was no hope for my father.

Information... does it help us or harm us? As a nurse, I have always thought that patients should be well-informed about their process, so that they can best respond to it. As painful as it is, disease gives us the opportunity to bring out the tools of personal power that we have inside us. I have witnessed many conspiracies of silence. It is quite common, especially when it is older relatives who are affected by the disease. In such cases, some members of the family, usually the elder's adult children, decide that the diagnosis is too hard for the elder to take and, moved by a desire to protect their loved one, they underestimate the patient's personal power and take on the role of a parent: "I will protect you and carry your suffering as well as mine on my back". Then there is the patient, playing the role of a helpless child who has no tools to cope with the situation and no personal power to use. This conspiracy of silence pattern takes up a great deal of energy as we try to hide reality from a "child" who usually ends up discovering it anyway. And it may happen that the elder, in turn, tries to conceal the fact that he or she knows the truth. So all the people involved wastes a huge amount of energy trying to hide "the secret" and a great hidden pain grows inside each of them.

I think it is important that the patient understand what is happening so that he or she can ask, with love: What is this ailment trying to tell me? What can I modify in myself to recover my physical and emotional health? And the answers will come. To ignore the disease will only make it grow, as it tries to get you to finally listen to what it wants to tell you.

How much should we know? I dislike prognoses, to me they seem cruel... To estimate the time a person has left to live can have a terrible impact, so much so that the person may be catapulted towards the expected demise. Some time ago a young person affected by melanoma (skin cancer) began receiving treatment at the medical center where I work. The patient had already completed the early stages of treatment and was set to begin the maintenance stage. The patient approached me to ask about the next appointment. I was holding the patient's records in my hands at the time and, when I checked the date of the next appointment, I saw that the patient, who was standing next to me, was staring right at the medical diagnosis: "Metastatic melanoma stage IV, poor prognosis". The patient left immediately, looking upset, obviously very much affected by the diagnosis-prognosis. That very afternoon the patient had a heart attack and died.

Information is good, because it enables you to look straight into the eyes of the ailment. It prepares you to use all your energy in the process of harnessing your inner power and commencing the healing. However, once we understand the ailment, I think it is not a good idea to wallow in the information, because this removes us from the healing process we want to initiate.

But let's return to my father's story, to my story. To confirm the diagnosis, we went to Gran Canaria to have my father seen at a hospital with greater human and material resources. There they performed more tests and suggested surgical resection as treatment. First it would be necessary to drain the bile accumulated in the liver, so as to reduce the jaundice. The morning of the surgery, in February of 2011, my father came out of the interventional radiology unit completely defeated. He did not have the strength to get out of bed, he had no appetite, he could barely speak and he was in severe pain, a situation that lasted over a week. The attempt to drain the liver had failed and the numerous stabs with the needle trying to drain it had

caused the tumor to disseminate. Two weeks later the doctors told us that the tumor had grown very quickly and that the portal vein that irrigates the liver was affected; the likelihood of survival was therefore even lower.

When the range of possibilities dwindles, you feel that a piece of life disappears with each hope that is eliminated. Hopes that you had placed... in what? In medical treatments that are going to lead you to survival? On this side of the world, when our chances of survival are no longer what had been "estimated" and when the options of surgery or pharmacological treatment become smaller, it seems we lose all hope. But what about the energy that you sent out into the universe so that your relative or you yourself could heal? Is that energy also lost with those "medical impossibilities"? Do we put all of our healing into the hands of doctors? Do we expect another person, whom we do not know and who does not know us, to tackle our disease process? We tend to say: "take my challenge, please fix it for me, because I am afraid to accept that there are emotions, environments, learned patterns, addictive behavior, anger, resentment, guilt... that I don't know how to handle". We act like children with no tools of our own and we need a doctor-parent who guides us down the path of our own healing.

I have often asked myself: What does it mean to accept? What does it encompass? The general definition is: "to regard as proper or to receive something voluntarily and without opposition". But what is it that we are accepting? If we live in a state of acceptance we open ourselves to trusting that the life process has brought us to this place for a reason, so that we can grow with the challenge, gain confidence in our own personal power and seek the full range of resources that can help us in

our healing process. The flip side of the same coin is resignation, since if
we resign ourselves to something we give permission to the patterns that
have governed us for years to keep steering the boat and believing that
they have won. We give them the reins of our personal power.

In my opinion, those of us who work in today's Western healthcare
systems do not really understand the difference between acceptance

and resignation. We believe that patients are *accepting* their process but
the fact is they are *resigned* to it. In contrast, some people really grow
inside as a result of the process, they open up to the idea of externalizing
their emotions, they begin to appreciate themselves, to forgive
themselves, to realize that the important thing in life is to enjoy the
moment, without worrying about the uncertain future and without
focusing on a possibly painful past. The challenge opens their eyes so
that they can begin to appreciate the reality of now. And although the
doctor may bring the news that the treatment options are limited,
people who respond this way have already connected with their internal
greatness and they feel so free that the blow is not so hard.

After news of the tumor's expansion, I, as the good oncology nurse that
I was, took on an attitude of resignation. However, in my family there
was one person who was not resigned, but rather was in acceptance
mode, and that was my mother: she was convinced that there were still
chances and that we had to find them. That is why ⊢—with the help of
the chief of surgery— in three weeks we were on our way to Barcelona,
with our hopes set on a complicated surgical intervention that could
save my father's life.

There everything happened very quickly: the operation was scheduled to
take place in one week. At that time I realized that life was being good to
us and I consciously said to myself: I am going to use all the tools I have
to ensure that this process in which my entire family is involved has a
happy ending. Days before the operation, my mother and I got to work:
we did Ho'oponopono, we visualized my father in a good state of health,
we consciously sent him loving energy, we channeled Reiki at the time
of the operation, we recited mantras... Both of us projected on him all
kinds of actions linked to energies with healing frequencies. Without us
realizing it, all of these actions brought greater consciousness to my

mother and I, opening up paths that were also connected to our own process of inner healing.

As for the patient's attitude, I can say that my father clearly manifested two realities: resignation and isolation. The result was loneliness, suffering, powerlessness.

What a wide variety of attitudes and behaviors a disease can manifest! In my view, many of these attitudes come from the beliefs we have held since childhood about illness, about the externalization of emotions and about the relationship of love we have with ourselves.

What is disease? For what reason or for what purpose does a disease appear? What does this disease give to me? These questions, and their answers, can determine the attitude of the sick person. Look to see if when you were little you were taught that disease is a vehicle with which to get attention, or if when you were sick you were isolated in the bedroom, or if you were overprotected and not allowed to do anything. Shedding light on these concepts and seeing that our behavioral patterns tend to repeat themselves will help us change our attitude and focus on healing. The externalization of our emotions and the way we manage each kind of emotion will condition disease processes. When an organ shouts out in pain, it is asking you to externalize something, through words, tears, laughter, or properly managed anger... It is saying "listen to me and speak for me" in no uncertain terms! Such liberation makes us aware that what we have been repressing for so many years is what was harming us. When you liberate it, the space freed up fills with love.

Throughout my professional career and personal life I have observed that aggressiveness, emotional instability, anxiety and depression are all signs that we are not managing the process well.

Greater and lesser degrees of aggressiveness are often expressed through words, gestures, attempts to attack using past issues that are unrelated, etc... Once when I asked a patient's wife about the scratches and bruises on her arms, she tearfully admitted: "My husband has been aggressive lately. The other day he tried to hit me for the first time in my life. He feels powerless". Feeling powerless is non-acceptance of the process and the refusal to look inside ourselves to find and manage our personal power.

In the cases of emotional instability, the person may become emotional for any sort of outside cause, as superfluous as it may seem, because for that person it is disproportionately symbolic. It is a form of emotional overflow. The person may not be manifesting their pain but the pain wants to seep out through any emotional crevice that activates it.

Throughout the disease process one of these sentiments may predominate (aggressiveness, emotional instability, anxiety and depression), or several might arise simultaneously.

It is important to consider the love relationship that we have with ourselves: how are we going to begin the healing process if we do not love ourselves? It would be a contradiction. Feeling love, compassion and a forgiving attitude towards ourselves enables us to connect directly with our tools of personal power.

The morning of March 2 my father was wheeled into the operating room. In the waiting room of that cold hospital, my mother and I recited the mantra of the Buddha of Medicine, we sent Reiki (to my father and to the doctors) and we visualized my father healthy and happy. By that afternoon he was in intensive care. Seven liver segments had been removed, of the nine that a healthy liver has; the small portion remaining was struggling to keep my father alive. We visited him every morning and afternoon during visiting hours and we used the time for the daily session of Reiki and Tibetan energy therapies. I could feel my own energy flow improving; I was receiving blessings and love from the universe... I felt fortunate. Five days after the operation he was progressing well and was taken back to his room. Three weeks later we returned to Lanzarote.

The motivation for inner work should come from the person who is sick. But we all have roles within the family structure and sometimes these roles are pathological or hinder such a process. We need to become aware of the roles we play in the family: illness is an opportunity to correct patterns that do not bring health and love. We must forgive. Our egos are absurd compared to the power of the disease and the possibility of death. We will then realize how much energy was wasted maintaining egotic structures that keep us away from our true nature. All that energy, when projected in a positive way and with true love toward our relative, can become a force for healing and transformation.

The return home was hard. Since January my father had been losing weight. He had lost about half of his normal weight and by the time we returned home he weighed just 100 lbs. Having such a low energy level and so little appetite, he stayed in bed practically all day long. Then, no more than five days after our return, he had to be re-admitted to the hospital. I remember those days as the hardest of all that we had gone through. Several tests were performed. The results confirmed that the tumor had reappeared but with the additional problem of acute sepsis. My father was semi-conscious, breathing with difficulty, wavering between life and death and, in fact, looking more dead than alive. The doctors said he probably would not last more than a few hours.

But this message did not resonate in me, nor did it resonate in my mother... Denial? I had used and heard that term so many times! But no, it was not denial. I accepted the situation and continued to do Reiki, recite mantras and send love. The afternoon he was admitted, a friend and co-worker came up to me and said: "Jeza, your father is going to die and I get the feeling you are not facing the reality that we all see". Her bluntness started me thinking about all those times in which the relatives of a patient on the brink of death would approach me and, to my great surprise, ask the following question: "Do you think he/she will make it through?" I also recalled all those times that I had said: "oh, there's no escape for that lady" or "she's almost at the door" as we say so casually in the healthcare profession. I became aware of the terrible energy burden that we are projecting on people with such messages.

But there are people who do overcome the disease when it looks like they are at death's door. Some beings connect with the drive for inner change that is welling up in them and they realize they can ke contributing things of value to the world, through love.

After three weeks of treatment with antibiotics and healing ener' father was still alive. We went back to the Barcelona hospit medical staff finished curing him of the sepsis and, surprisingly, was found to be healthy. Not a trace of the tumor! Today the l grown to twice the size it was then and my father is perfectly healthy. Life has given us, my father and the family, another opportunity.

It's funny but when a disease process is underway, we don't notice the changes that are taking place in us and in the family structure. Only now, a year and a half after the complicated intervention, am I beginning to understand the profound meaning of this disease, the lessons it taught me. I imagine that every person and every family, in their personal circumstances and with their particular idiosyncrasies, will be able to understand this if they truly want to grow with the process.

Now I can think about what the teachings were for me...

I came to understand that for some reason my father was present and at the same time absent during many of the big events in my life. "Unconscious isolation" or at least that is how I felt it and experienced it. His illness was important in helping me to put him in the place he deserved to be.

I came to understand that for a long time I did not consider my family to be an open and safe setting for expressing my emotions, for communicating about the issues that were truly important and had emotional repercussions on me. I came to see that, due to certain conducts learned and perceived inside the family, I cut myself off from others, because I was afraid of being judged and not accepted.

I came to understand that we make judgments about the processes of other beings, whatever their challenge may be (a disease, a separation, a personal conflict...) and that, in addition, we have an influence on them in terms of energy. We often underestimate the personal power and the projection that this being wants to have on his or her life or process, whatever it may be.

I came to understand that the family structure is an entity in and of itself. As the holistic concept goes, it is "much more than the sum of its parts". This is important because, when one of the parts becomes ill, the family as a whole becomes ill. Observing our reactions and emotions and those of other members of the family provides a great deal of information about the fears, behaviors, and the learned and perceived beliefs in our family.

I came to understand that we are afraid to look inside ourselves and love ourselves just as we are at this precise moment. We are always postponing this task for "later on" when life, through the major challenges we face, is telling us "Now is the time". I learned that we can connect firmly with this intention of loving oneself from the perspective of "now".

I came to understand that, generally-speaking, we give our personal power to forces outside of us that we think can save us. If we believe in "something" or in "someone" we are placing our faith in that something or someone. And what if we put our faith in ourselves? In the end, everything and all of us come from the same original source that made life possible.

I came to understand that I choose to accept each process and change in my life as an opportunity to keep learning.

I came to understand that often we are determined to invest our own energy (as well as the energy of others) in the "healing" process of another person. But we must acknowledge that healing as we understand it on a material, or physical, plane is different from the "healing" that can happen on a spiritual plane. There may be times in which it is better to let our loved ones transcend and reconnect with life through death. We need to project far-reaching desires for "healing" without limiting ourselves to the purely physical sphere The universal intelligence above us knows the best fate for our soul.

I came to understand all of this... And I will no doubt gradually learn much more...

Thank you father, mother, sister, daughter... Thank you to those who were there and also to those who were not there.

See you soon!

"Although nobody can go back and get a new beginning,
anybody can start now and get a new ending".

Roberto Pérez

Dear reader,

Thank you for coming with me on this journey that has taken us through such an array of stories, reflections, practices... They have all been experienced and confirmed by me, and they have enabled me (and many others) to connect with the essence and to experience unshakeable happiness.

Now that we have reached this point, allow me to suggest something that I often suggest at the beginning of my workshops and gatherings. What I say is this: don't believe any of it! Simply go out and experience it for yourself!

Just a few weeks before I finished writing this book, a meditation student of mind who lost her 4-year-old son to cancer a few years ago said to me gratefully:

Now I can say from experience that we are all one. I close my eyes and feel it in my heart, and I see that my son is here with me, that he never left me. This makes me very happy.

My guiding sentiment has always been "Always learning, always sharing".

Remember: to become truly happy you don't need to have been born in Tibet or in India. You don't even need to give yourself an exotic name! There is just one thing you have to do: make PEACE your priority.

Thank you very, very much!

José Antonio Manchado

For more information and additional tools:

www.seamasfelizqueeldalailama.com
www.behappierthanthedalailama
www.joseantoniomanchado.com
www.facebook.com/seamasfelizqueeldalailama

About the author

José Antonio Manchado was born in Lanzarote (Canary Islands, Spain) in 1976.

Since 1999 he has been engaged in ongoing study and practice with several teachers (monks and lamas of the Buddhist, Tibetan and Zen traditions) in the fields of meditation, healing, sound and energy and vibrational therapies.

He currently spends his time sharing the wisdom and tools that transformed his life, teaching courses and workshops, giving lectures, offering meditation retreats and organizing other events focusing on mental, physical and spiritual well-being.